Jesus is knocking. Are you going to answer? Sabrina Fairchild gives you the keys to unlock a personal relationship with Christ. Whether you are new in your walk or further down the road, *Faith and the S.T.O.P. Principle* encourages you to open that door. He's waiting for you!

—Bethany Kole,
West End CRC Worship Committee Member

Faith and the S.T.O.P. Principle is a reflection of the author's humble relationship with Jesus Christ, giving glory to Him for His wonderful grace and mercy, and the thrill of going all out for His plan and purpose in life.

—Margaret Soderholm, Celebration Church
Women's Intercessory Prayer and Bible Study Leader

In *Faith and the S.T.O.P. Principle,* Sabrina shows us in a very simple, open, honest, forthright way how to have a relationship with the Creator of the universe, and then live every step of our journey, with God's Word as our guide.

—Helen Stewart,
Calvary Church Celebration Bible Study Teacher

FAITH AND THE
S.T.O.P.
PRINCIPLE

SABRINA FAIRCHILD

FAITH AND THE
S.T.O.P.
PRINCIPLE

LEARNING TO
SURRENDER, **T**RUST, **O**BEY, AND **P**ATIENTLY
WAIT UPON THE LORD

TATE PUBLISHING & *Enterprises*

Published by Tate Publishing & Enterprises, LLC
127 E. Trade Center Terrace | Mustang, Oklahoma 73064 USA
1.888.361.9473 | www.tatepublishing.com

Tate Publishing is committed to excellence in the publishing industry. The company reflects the philosophy established by the founders, based on Psalm 68:11,
"The Lord gave the word and great was the company of those who published it."

Book design copyright © 2010 by Tate Publishing, LLC. All rights reserved.
Cover design by Jeff Fisher
Interior design by Joey Garrett

Published in the United States of America

ISBN: 978-1-61663-543-5
1. Religion / Christian Life / General
2. Religion / Christian Life / Spiritual Growth
10.08.31

DEDICATION

I believe *Faith and the S.T.O.P. Principle* was laid upon my heart by God. His message today is the same as it was in the garden of Eden—to follow Him. In John 6:29, Jesus answered a crowd of followers who had asked what they needed to do to do the works God required by saying, "The work of God is this: to believe in the one he has sent." I believe in Christ with all my heart, and dedicate this book to Him. May salvation be yours when you ask to receive the same promise of life that He has given me.

ACKNOWLEDGMENTS

My sister, Stacey, would tell you that she has little to offer outside her love for others, and then she quickly corrects herself by saying that all of her qualities are blessings from God. She never takes credit for His glory.

I'm third in line for knowing her the longest (outside of my parents and eldest sister), which has been my entire life. In that time I have watched a tenderhearted child develop into a truth-seeking, Christ follower. She has surrendered her whole heart over to Him, and He clearly dwells in her. First John 3:23–24 says, "And this is his command: to believe in the name of his Son, Jesus Christ, and to love one another as he commanded us. Those who obey his commands live in him, and he in them. And this is how we know that he lives in us: We know it by the Spirit he gave us."

Stacey has taught me so many valuable lessons like

how to treat others with respect regardless of their manner, how to humble yourself before the Lord in both suffering and times of joy. Most of all, she stands firm in the truth of God's Word by taking responsibility for her words and behavior. Sin is not a pretty sight, but God offers a way from under it through the shed blood of His Son. There's such freedom in repentance, and so few choose it.

Thank you, Sta, for being my childhood bunk bed buddy and lifelong playmate. You are a blessing and tremendous role model. I hope you don't mind me sharing your favorite verse and motto: "And we know that in all things God works for the good of those who love him, who have been called according to his purpose" (Romans 8:28).

God rocks!

TABLE OF CONTENTS

FOREWORD

This book is so clearly the work of the Holy Spirit, and this foreword is truly an act of the Holy Spirit. It is so very exciting and awe inspiring to know that He has made all of this come to fruition. I am humbled to be a part of it, and to God be all the honor and glory.

I would have to say that about fifteen years ago (and many times thereafter) God used me to plant a seed in Sabrina. I knew without a doubt she needed to write a book. If she had written it back then, it would not have been the one you are about to read. Praise God and His perfect timing! He had some incredible experiences and life altering trials for Him to take her through before He could use her to write *Faith and the S.T.O.P. Principle.* I can attest to the amazing journey she's been on and how God has used it in writing this book. Over and over again, I have come back to Romans 8:28: "And we know that in all things God works for the good of those who love him, who have been called according to his purpose." He has so greatly proven this verse in Sabrina's life. As you read this book and, in turn, apply the S.T.O.P. Principle to your life, keep Romans 8:28 fresh in your mind. You too will be awestruck by God's promise in it and your surrendered life. It doesn't matter where you are or what you are going through at this very moment—God can use whatever it is for your ultimate good and His honor and glory.

I pray that the Holy Spirit uses *Faith and the S.T.O.P. Principle* in a mighty way in your walk with Jesus Christ. Your walk with Him is everything. He is absolutely everything and you can trust Him with every area of your life.

Stacey Lynn Pattegar

INTRODUCTION: TEARS OF JOY

LEARN TO DEVELOP YOUR TEARS OF JOY THROUGH THIS BOOK

Jesus wept, right? And Scripture tells us that He cried over *one of us:* Lazarus, a dear friend and child of God.

So why do I cry every time I hear *His Name?* While sitting in the congregation of my church recently, I recalled a story of a philosophy professor at one of the prestigious universities of our fine country, and the only question during the Blue Book part of the exam was: Why? While all of the students furiously wrote their answers in the time remaining, one student simply answered, "Why not?" He scored one hundred percent!

Recalling this somewhat humorous tale, I looked up and saw the Hebrew word for God, YHWH, dangling from a mobile hung from the sanctuary ceiling. A word so holy around the time God's temple was being rebuilt in Israel that saying it publicly was forbidden.

Backwards, YHWH spells HWHY. This may be a stretch for you, but it seems like every time something goes wrong, I inevitably ask the Lord, "Why?" And during a somewhat quiet part of the service, I nearly jumped out of my pew to exclaim the answer: Holy God is WHY! Forward or backward, YHWH is the one true answer: God, Holy God.

is for
YHWH (LORD)

God desires to make His name known.

Isaiah 42:8a
I am the LORD; that is My name.

Psalm 9:10a
Those who know Your name will trust in You.

Artwork by Storm

TWELVE WEEKS TO
STARTING TO S.T.O.P.

During the next twelve weeks, you will start assessing your spiritual walk with the Lord. The goal is to get into the Word and learn how to *surrender* control, *trust* God in all things, know when He is leading you to act in *obedience* to His will and *patiently* wait for His timing to be revealed in your life.

This process may bring you to tears a time or two! However, if you choose to apply the S.T.O.P. Principle to your faith in Christ, you will begin to notice your tears of frustration developing into tears of joy. I indiscriminately cry so much that people either look away or they inquire, "What's the matter?" The truthful answer to what is who. Then I really get the stares—blank ones!

You see, who is the Holy Spirit, whom filled my entire being at the moment I accepted Jesus as Savior (1 John 4:13). At the mere utterance of Christ's name, my eyes well up with tears as the Holy Spirit moves me in praise and reverence to God. I am in constant awe of His provision, promises, and love.

We live in a time when everyone wants to put a label on anything from our feelings to a reason that dismisses our bad behavior. I've been told that I'm being convicted or asked what I have done wrong. Yes, the Holy Spirit does convict us, and it can often times be an extremely emotional and difficult experience; however, I'm convinced that my tears that cause others discomfort are a result of tears of joy.

With joy, there is no sadness. Joy is a fruit of the

Spirit and is mentioned in both the Old and New Testaments 237 times! It is these tears that I'd like to examine so you and I can go before the Lord as one body completed in His love.

HOW TO DRENCH YOURSELF IN THIS STUDY GUIDE

Sharing your walk with others is an essential part of building the body of Christ. Before you get started, pair up with an accountability partner within your study group. Choose five to ten questions, per couple, to study and pray over throughout the week. When you come together as a group, try reviewing all of the answers for the entire chapter. This method will help you stay focused on Christ, build godly friendships, and to see how God works in and through you!

I humbly thank you for walking through my aches and victories in the pages to follow. Hopefully, you will relate a little, grow a bit, and cry out to Jesus a lot! He's waiting for you to love Him with all you've got!

PART ONE

I'M IN CONTROL

Life is tough. On any given day, my routine requires getting up too early in the morning and going to bed too late at night. I'm willing to concede that your routine is probably similar. I'm not alone in feeling this way, I know, but at least I'm somewhat in control of how everything plays out each day.

Early on in my career, I was stalked by a co-worker. At that point in my life, I was pretty trusting of people but not anymore. I go out of my way to either take a different route to work or make sure I'm the first one who leaves an event so no one can follow me home! So far, my strategy has worked, and I haven't been harassed by anyone since. You learn quickly when someone infringes upon your privacy. Maybe you can relate to this too.

As a single homeowner, I end up taking on quite a few household chores I normally wouldn't have to if

I were married (or would I?). Like fixing the outdoor light, caulking a window, heavy yard work, or maintaining the car. It seems like everything depends on me, and most days I wish it were just the opposite. It would be nice to be able to count on someone to take over where I leave off or to simply do it all! But I'm just dreaming. There's no such promise in this life. Right?

EVERYTHING DEPENDS ON ME

For many years I had this attitude and didn't even know it! It wasn't until God literally spoke to me one morning that I was awakened to my wrong choice of attitude. The Lord said, "Sabrina, nothing depends on you or anyone else. Everything depends on Me." His clear words were the beginning of my changed behavior.

All of a sudden, I started to think of all the times I had taken control of a situation by talking my way through it. Never once did I go to God in prayer until *after* each task was completed. Who do you suppose this made the most happy? You got it; Satan! Satan was at the root of all I had done wrong because I fell into his subtle trap and lie that I was capable to make things happen on my own! Since reconciling with God about my all consuming independence, I can't help but see how many others are living the same lie. As a result, there is a growing population of self-made, self-sufficient, self-serving, self-centered, selfish people!

Getting back to what God said to me about depending on Him for all things, I know you're saying, "Wow, what a promise!" But you're also probably wondering how I knew that God was really speaking to me. There are two ways of determining the source of your thoughts. The first is asking God to give you peace with what you just heard. If you suddenly feel uneasy, then it was not of God. Second, get out your Bible and start looking for scripture that confirms the truth. The Bible is full of promises and will never lead you or me astray! In this case, Romans 8:28 popped into my head and reads, "And we know that in all things God works for the good of those who love him, who have been called according to his purpose." Can you imagine? All of us were purposely created by God. He has a plan for our lives, and all we have to do is love and depend on Him!

Lately, there have been national news reports that claim there is an all-time high number of people who claim to be atheists. Of course, one has to believe there's a God to deny Him, right? Maybe that's just me, but my other observation is this: why atheism? Of all things to believe in this world and the choice is self? Has living become so unattractive that all we have to look forward to is what we can provide on our own? And since we're talking amongst ourselves, is depending on self possible when the Bible claims God to be the ultimate authority of mankind?

Let's take a look for a minute and see what I mean by that question. In Revelation 6:15, we learn:

> Then the kings of the earth, the princes, the gener-

als, the rich, the mighty, and every slave and every free man hid in caves and among the rocks of the mountains. They called to the mountains and the rocks, "Fall on us and hide us from the face of him who sits on the throne and from the wrath of the Lamb! For the great day of their wrath has come, and who can stand?"

Isn't this cool stuff? God appears to be in control! Unbelievers (those who were not raptured before or born during the tribulation) try to flee the sight of the Lord, but they can't get away! God is everywhere or omnipresent. No one, no matter how much or how little he or she has in life, can hide from His sight. Therefore, all are forced to acknowledge His presence and existence as the one and only living God! As a matter of a fact, the verse ends with the unbelieving kings to slaves talking to a bunch of rocks and begging the mountains and rocks to fall on them so they don't have to face Jesus!

Can anyone claim to not believe in God when His Word says otherwise? It seems to me that yes, we all have the *temporary* free will to deny God and His Son, but scripture promises that there will come a time that we *all* have to face Him. So why avoid living in harmony with our Creator here and now when we know how everything is going to end? What could possibly be so worthwhile that doing things our way is better than His?

Sadly, I spent several years going it alone all the while telling myself that I was being obedient to God's will. Are you starting to discover the same tendencies in your life? Although I called myself a believer, I was constantly guilty of stealing God's glory by living as if everything was a result of my hard work! I'm so excited to share that I no longer live this way and hope you decide to join me. If you're ready to turn your back on the person who would rather talk to rocks and instead learn how to build a rock solid relationship with the One who laid down His life for you, then keep reading!

CHRIST ROCKS!

Okay, forgive me for twisting the ironic to make a bigger point, because building a relationship with Christ really does rock! And if you were kind of on the fence about whether or not you wanted to talk to the rocks that are mentioned in Revelation (all prophecy *will be fulfilled* and unbelievers will indeed plead with them), keep this in mind: Jesus is literally *the* Rock. Second Samuel 22:47 says, "The Lord lives! Praise be to my Rock! Exalted be God, the Rock, my Savior!" First Corinthians 10:4 is equally interesting as the Apostle Paul tells the new believers of Corinth, "...for they drank from the spiritual rock that accompanied them, and that rock was Christ."

How about that? The very rocks that unbelievers beg to fall upon and cover them from the face of God is the Rock of salvation, the living God, Jesus Christ! Rocks are significant in scripture and either have eyes (Zechariah 3:9) or God uses them to provide water to His people in their time of need (Isaiah 48:21).

Moreover, the Rock of salvation will talk to you

when you talk to Him! Outside of being forgiven of your sins, communicating with Christ is one of the greatest benefits of having a personal relationship with Him. No longer will you go numb asking random rocks to hide you because the One who offers salvation is waiting to be your personal cornerstone!

Choosing to have a relationship with Christ is the single most important decision you will ever make. It has eternal value. If you can get over the hurdle of what and whom you believe in, by coming to the conclusion that Jesus is *the* Rock instead of *a* rock, then you are well on your way to a fulfilling life in Him.

King Solomon is the wisest man of all time, and in Proverbs 28:25–26 he writes, "A greedy man stirs up dissension, but he who trusts in the Lord will prosper. He who trusts in himself is a fool, but he who walks in wisdom is kept safe." I'd like to be safe, and I surely don't want to be a fool. Accepting Christ into your heart is the equivalent of being led to the knowledge of the truth (Colossians 1:9–14). You and I may not come up with all of the answers in the pages of this book, but the wisdom of God's Word does, along with a promise to safely lead us in our daily walk.

I DON'T KNOW HOW TO HAVE A RELATIONSHIP WITH CHRIST

Neither did I, at first. We all say we don't know how to have a personal relationship with Christ, and for many of us, we never truly try to know Him. We think that having a relationship with the One who claims to be fully God and fully Man is going to make us change the way we live. Or worse yet, we may have to go to someone and admit that we were wrong about something!

To intimately know Christ requires a focus adjustment and at least three things immediately take place: (1) a transition from trying to control your circumstances to recognizing all things go through Him first, (2) surrendering said control over to Him each and every day and, (3) a *desire* to change to be more like Him. A sure sign that all three of these actions are taking root is the understanding that when you're not in a trial, God is most likely preparing you for one and that each change helps us grow in His Spirit. This is God's way of building trust, drawing us near and refining us into the image of Christ.

Accepting Christ and living for Christ are different choices. The former leads to two separate paths: pursuing an intimate relationship or putting God in a box. Pursuing an intimate relationship teaches us *how to live* for Christ and is exactly what God intended for all believers. You may be stumbling along the second path (putting God in a box) if you have found that you're no further in your relationship than you were the day you invited Jesus into your heart.

This is where transformation comes into play. It is the desire to align yourself with God's will and therefore put Christ at the center of your prayers, thoughts, and actions. Choosing to do anything outside of Christ has the dangerous potential to put your wants (notice I didn't say needs) ahead of the plans and purpose God has for your life. It is competition for the throne that

Christ rightfully deserves. You need to ask yourself how much room you're willing to give, and if the answer isn't one hundred percent, then you may need to do some serious soul searching about who has priority in your life. There are only two options: Christ or self.

It's frustrating not to see progress in a relationship, especially when the other person is hard to track down. Imagine how God feels when we put Him on a shelf and say, "I don't have any spare time right now, but I'll be sure to call on you when I'm in trouble!" We all do it, and it's not right. At some point, you need to decide how much truth you want to live and make a commitment to love Christ with all your heart, all your mind, and all your strength!

Another hurdle involves answering the age-old question: where do I begin? The best advice I can give you right now is to say that getting to know Christ will take you the rest of your life and into eternity to fully know Him! There isn't a college course or book, including the Bible, that can contain Him. He is the Alpha and the Omega, the Beginning and the End, the Truth, Life, and Light. Each time I meet someone new, I want to know as much about him or her as I possibly can! So get started by treating Christ like you would any new relationship. Since He's the well-known Author of creation and is quoted in the Bible, then start reading His Book. When you go to Him in prayer, either ask questions and wait for His answers or read passages from His Word and see where He leads you in scripture. Are you starting to picture how this relationship works? It's personal, so treat it as such.

If you're okay with just getting by in the faith department and have to ask the question, "Does God really have something to do with absolutely everything?" then you are in denial of what it is to surrender your life over to God. The truth is once you accept Christ as Savior, you no longer desire to depend on your own devices; rather you start letting go of your former way of living. Depending on Christ means living for Him and not for what you or the world has to offer. Now I'm not saying that you don't continue pursuing an education or making a living, but what I am saying is that you no longer are blazing your own trail; instead Jesus is lighting the path for you!

Blazing your own trail involves reliance upon your sin nature. Allowing Jesus to lead the way is where the Spirit comes into your life. For those of you who think visually, this will make a whole lot of sense when we dig deeper in You, Yourself, and Him in Part Three. Once through the material, hopefully you will be skipping along the narrow path!

RELATIONSHIPS ARE HARD WORK!

I can honestly say that I have never given up on learning how to have a relationship with Christ; I simply went about it the wrong way. Looking back, it's obvious that I wasn't studying the Scriptures like I knew I should have been. Part of the reason for my own denial was because I didn't feel worthy of interpreting scripture. Getting over that fear through prayer and finding a good study Bible helped me tremendously. You can and need to do the same.

At one point, prayer was not my friend. As you can imagine, the premise of prayer isn't about friendship but rather relationship. I was treating my prayer life in the same manner I was handling my stage-one relationship with Christ. Neither are machines that produce a certain feeling or product, but I was determined to put forth little genuine effort with great hopes of a huge benefit or return! Once I learned that prayer is a lifestyle and choice to whole-heartedly, humbly submit myself before the Lord, then I was able to receive God's blessings, as well as hear when He was calling or specifically answering my prayers and petitions. Heard prayers require a personal heart change so the Holy Spirit can communicate through a mutually loving relationship.

I also didn't understand what it meant to completely surrender control of my life over to God. When I was on my knees about something challenging, I vowed to handle it God's way, but as soon as I was through the fire, I was back to normal living! That's called a bad habit, not surrender. Surrender is so important and requires complete dependence upon the Lord.

The opposite of control is faith, and it is our faith in Christ that teaches us complete surrender. First, we must profess our faith in Christ. Once we've dedicated our hearts to Jesus, there are four crucial principles to building a healthy, intimate relationship with Him. The acronym I use is S.T.O.P. for surrender, trust, obedience, and patience. Stop generally implies not going any further, but in this case it is an encouragement to stop doing things as you have in the past and to start in a new direction, using the basic tools of spirituality.

Building relationships is a time-consuming affair; however, we were made to have them and Jesus came to show us how! You would think that we wouldn't need the help, but relationships can be complicated, yet rewarding. What's comforting is knowing that God doesn't ask us to do anything Jesus hasn't already done. He is the example we can count on to get it right every time.

The basis of any relationship is love. Since God is love and Jesus commands us to love one another so that the world may know that we are of Him, then we need to work on loving one another (John 15:17)! Love conquers all, right? It covers over a multitude of sins (James 5:20).

I think the greatest challenge outside of surrendering complete control of your life over to Christ is making yourself available for others to love you. It sounds strange when it's put into words, but ponder that thought for a moment—putting your heart on a platter for others to share puts you in a vulnerable position. Our human nature is to protect our heart by putting up walls or setting boundaries, not offering it in its complete form.

When you start feeling insecure, remember to go back to what I said about God not asking us to do anything Jesus hasn't already done before us. Christ is our role model. Surrendering our hearts to Him is exactly what He did for the Father to redeem us. Jesus was crucified for His unconditional love for us. Ask

Jesus how to love as He loves us and others. Ask Him to soften your heart and lift the veil of darkness that is keeping you from unconditionally loving others. If Jesus commanded us to love, then He will give us the grace to do it!

The exciting part about depending upon the Lord for all things is seeing how He is changing your heart in order for you to obediently follow His commands. It's like an intricately woven heirloom doily that takes precision, love, passion, and a significant investment of your time. Once completed, it lasts for generations to come, the righteous fruit of your labor.

Giving of yourself also challenges our sin nature. We are told a lie that we need to take care of ourselves first and then the needs of others and only if we get that far! God's Word tells us time and again that we should live the complete opposite and follow the example Christ set for us. He left His Spirit as a deposit in us to guide our every move and counsel us in each decision we make. Give up that lie and invite Jesus to lead you in having deeper, more fulfilling relationships with those you love.

EVERYTHING DEPENDS ON HIM

I thank the Lord for His patience with me. I spent countless years pursuing a personal relationship with Christ but never quite matured enough spiritually to experience a full transformation. Roadblocks created out of my tendency to depend on self rather than God were the most harmful. Man-made rules, otherwise known as legalism, also held me down. I couldn't seem to separate the rules of old from the relationship Christ shed His blood to provide. How sad my life had become as I failed to meet the incessant expectations of this world when all along Jesus was right beside me, holding an open door to a new life in Him.

Yes, I believed in and accepted Him as my Savior many years before, but I never completely trusted Him at His Word to walk *through* the door. Until you walk through the same door that I finally accepted as the Truth and the Way, you will also remain in a perpetual state of confusion about where you stand in relationship with an all-knowing, always present, and all-powerful God.

Throughout the course of this book, I'd like to share with you a handful of the spiritually life-altering trials God used to get my attention. I'm humbled by His all encompassing love, grace, and mercy, and hope you choose to experience the same in your relationship.

God will never force a relationship but will knock until you answer Him one way or the other (Matthew 7:7, Luke 11:9). He will never stop pursuing you but will turn you over to what you ask. Jesus is the only name under heaven that can wash us clean and make us whole before the Father (Acts 4:12). The day you choose to depend on Christ for all things is the day you are free from the bondage of sin! I have and not only live as though everything depends on Him; I count on it!

It's time to dig a little deeper, and you may have noticed that some of the sections have up to twenty questions or more to answer. Get into the practice of being in the very good company of others and pair up with someone within your Bible study to be your accountability partner! Each week, divide the questions amongst yourselves and plan to discuss them prior to meeting with your group. This method will accomplish two things: (1) take away the obligation of *getting through* the questions and allow you to spend more time on the one's you have selected and (2) build a new friendship. For those of you who are thirsting for a more intimate relationship with Christ, please consider answering *all* of the questions. Each one is intended to help get the focus off of self and onto Him.

STUDY QUESTIONS

1. During any given day, do you feel more in or out of control of your life?

2. If everything depends on you, then whom do you trust in your darkest hour?

3. According to Romans 8:28, those who love God also have a God-given purpose. What is yours?

4. Have you ever had a time in your life when you tried to hide from God? Were you successful?

5. Only one question in our lifetime has eternal value attached to the answer. What is the question we must all answer?

6. How have you pursued *relating* to Christ?

7. What three things happen when you put your focus on Christ?

8. Is *living for* Christ the same as *accepting* Christ as Savior?

9. What does transformation mean?

10. If God is on your shelf, who or what are you giving priority?

11. What is required of you to ask Christ to be your personal Savior?

12. Describe what happens to your heart once you choose Christ.

13. Define surrender.

14. What is the opposite of faith?

15. Why was Jesus crucified?

16. Have man-made rules paved your path to relationship or rebellion?

17. What do you think will happen if you decide to completely depend on Christ?

WHO I AM

My parents say I was a happy baby. Content is the word they used to describe my overall mannerisms, and now they both agree that I walk to the beat of a different drummer! I take all of it as a compliment even though I feel like they don't have the first clue as to what that phrase means. Dad says it means that I'm independent, different, unique, and that he sees it as a good quality. Our whole conversation makes me kind of chuckle because I'm not sure if he was convincing himself that I'm okay or if he was trying to make me feel better for saying that I'm out there!

Who I am is how God made me. In Psalm 139, David excitedly describes how the Lord has searched him and knows him. In verse two, he says, "You know when I sit and when I rise; you perceive my thoughts from afar." Scroll down to verse 13, and like a Shakespearean poem, he says, "For you created my inmost being; you knit me together in my mother's womb." Most important to this amazing visual of God's love for His creation follows in verse 14 as David professes, "I praise you because I am fearfully and wonderfully made; your works are wonderful, I know that full well."

Mind you, David doesn't say that he is made perfect. He simply praises the Lord for who he is and is *content* with how God made him. How many of us praise God each day for the way He has made us?

The Old Testament is originally written in Hebrew. According to my text, *inmost being* is a Hebrew idiom referring to the center of emotions and moral sensitivity. What I like about understanding the root words in Scripture is that it all means something specific about how we were made to worship God. It is our very core that seeks a relationship with Him, whether we're aware of it or not.

Did you know that a mother's womb is a secret place? Bible scholars compare the womb to the depths of the earth. That's who Jesus is to me when I need shelter from the world around me. I can go to Him for anything, anytime, and He is always near to hear my call.

I was born in Pontiac, Michigan, on the east side of the state outside of Detroit. My father worked for General Motors and made the long drive into work each day while my mother and two older sisters went about our daily routine of going to school, doing homework, and playing outside.

We had a great house on a small lake that was like a wonderland for fishing, swimming, water skiing, and in the winter, ice skating! If my mom would have let me, I would've pitched a tent near the lakeshore and slept outdoors so I could hear the birds chirp and weeping willows creak throughout the night.

Music has always been a huge part of my life. When I was four, my parents started me taking violin lessons using the Suzuki method. I learned how to play by ear before I was old enough to learn how to sight-read. Listening became so natural that I faked everything else, and to this day I still cannot read a single note. What I mean by faking is that I could play anything after hearing it one time. I performed solo in the church band, was selected to play for the Oklahoma Junior Symphony, and joined my college orchestra. At each audition, I either overheard the person before me or asked someone to play a few bars of the part I was supposed to sight-read and then repeated what I heard to make the final cut. Sounds make sense to me. It's like I know the next note before its time, and the music rolls off my strings, like a sand piper gracefully glides over the whitecaps along Lake Michigan on a breezy, summer afternoon.

The best way I know how to express my thoughts and feelings is through playing the violin, singing, whistling, talking, or writing. One time, I asked to call my grandmother just so I could let her hear that I had just learned how to whistle!

My mom is a piano player, and my two sisters are musical too! Shelly is a flutist, and Stacey plays classical guitar. Lessons, practice, and recitals were commonplace in our household. My mom was also a part of a trio that traveled from church to church, and oftentimes we girls would come along to accompany them in some form or fashion. My sisters and I also joined various choirs, whether at school or through church-related youth programs.

Where's my dad in all of this? He was the sound guy and was always engineering a better way to record us during our recitals or outside performances. Basically, he did the best he could with a primitive microphone and tape recorder!

RULES V. RELATIONSHIP

The dynamics of our household seemed pretty consistent as far as my older sister, Shelly, always had her own room while Stacey and I shared. In no time, we became bunk bed buddies, and when I wasn't whistling, we were both flapping our jaws about anything and everything. Not a night went by without us getting yelled at to "be quiet and go to sleep!"

Our weekends were pretty routine as well. On Fridays we would go out to eat at one of our family hot spots. If nothing else, dinner was a prelude to Saturday chores that would make a grown man cry. I can remember countless trips to the local hardware store to pick up supplies to either repair or build something that usually required heavy lifting, loud sawing, and hours upon hours of standing around! Dad liked to make a mess, and Mom loved to complain about how we all tracked sawdust into her newly cleaned house. Let's not forget about yard work that included mowing, trimming by hand (of course), and raking pine needles along the side of the house.

Once the work was done, then we could play. I have fond memories of tearing down to the lake and jumping off the dock into the cool water or taking a quick boat ride.

Sunday was spent either attending church or resting, as God commands us. Following the rules was a big part of my upbringing, especially when it came to resting on the Sabbath; no one dared to lift a finger.

Resting in the Lord through prayer and His Word is an essential part of building our relationship with God, but there is no longer a rule that it has to be on the Sabbath. Instead believers are free to worship when they choose because the Holy Spirit lives in us at all times and not just on Sunday. Paul clears up a lot of questions I had as a kid about the rules of having a personal relationship with Christ. In Colossians 2, he teaches that the day Christ sacrificed his life we were no longer bound by man-made rules, rituals, or religion:

> When you were dead in your sins and in the uncircumcision of your sinful nature, God made you alive with Christ. He forgave us all our sins, having canceled the written code, with its regulations, that was against us and that stood opposed to us; he took it away, nailing it to the cross. And having disarmed the powers and authorities, he made a public spectacle of them, triumphing over

them by the cross. Therefore do not let anyone judge you by what you eat or drink, or with regard to a religious festival, a New Moon celebration or a Sabbath day. These are a shadow of the things that were to come; the reality, however, is found in Christ.

Colossians 2:13–17

We are no longer separated from God but reconciled to Him by the shed blood of Jesus. In the Old Testament, there were three Judaic laws that included civil, ceremonial, and God's moral Law handed down in the form of the Ten Commandments. According to Romans 6:14–15, believers are under grace, not law, because the law doesn't have the power to release us from our sin. Instead we are slaves to righteousness! In Christ we are no longer bound to the ceremonial and civil laws; however, we do continue to follow the Ten Commandments out of obedience to God and because they were personally handed down to us by God. Jesus even teaches us about the Law in Matthew 5:17–20 and is clear that we are to continue following the Ten Commandments until He returns for us! (Samra 2009)

I began learning about Jesus in Sunday school and remember asking a lot of questions about His character. It seemed strange that someone I never met wrote about creating and loving me in a book called the Bible. I became a human sponge and learned that

Christ is God's only Son and that He is perfect, blameless, and the Word in flesh. I was comforted to hear of His unconditional love, and my Sunday school teachers said that God loved me so much that He sent Jesus to save me from all the bad choices I have and will make throughout my life.

When I was about seven years old, I remember asking my dad to help me pray for Jesus to come into my heart. What a glorious memory. At the time, I was sleeping in the lower bunk bed as Dad confirmed that I understood what it meant to repent and believe that Christ died on the cross to pay my sin debt in full. "Yes, Daddy," I said, and we both prayed together as I professed my faith.

My life instantly changed, but I was not yet transformed.

During the fifth and sixth grades, I was ready to write my first book! I loved Jesus so much and was particularly thankful that He had spared my life two years earlier and wanted to share my testimony with the world. Doctors had diagnosed and treated me for a one-time grand mal seizure, the result of rapid growth on one side of my brain.

It happened in the middle of the night while my dad was battling a mean headache. He says he got up to get an aspirin when he heard me flailing around in my bunk bed. I was still seizing while being rushed to the hospital for treatment. For a month, I was tested and retested before the doctor sent me home. He prescribed an experimental adult drug that almost immediately caused a violent reaction. Thank the Lord my parents were closely monitoring my progress because shortly after we got home I had to be rushed back to the hospital. Later, my mom learned that had they waited an hour, they would've lost me. My recovery took another two months before I was sent home for good.

Doesn't that sound like a great plot for a book? Since I was twelve at the time, I thought I'd make it a children's book and get plenty of press for being such a young author (not a bad marketing ploy!). Yet the real angle was that I was convinced God spared my life for something awesome. I just didn't know what He had in store or how He could use someone like me.

I had a lot of fun trying to get started. My mom let me borrow the typewriter she used in college, the non-electric kind, and I used construction paper because I wanted the pages to look pretty! Of course, that would have worked out well if I knew how to type and didn't need to use correction tape—yes, I said correction tape—to blot out all of the mistakes. I soon realized that handwriting was much more efficient and ditched the machine for a ballpoint pen!

Just when those creative juices were flowing, I'd be called to the dinner table or to do dishes. Attending school slowed me down a bit too. So I devised a plan to work with a co-author, my best friend, Gina. We could get twice as much done in the same amount of time and compare notes during class.

It was a great plan until I noticed that I couldn't read my own writing after stuffing the perfectly folded pages into my hot, sweaty, knee-high boots! It didn't help that my teacher caught me passing a note in class and stole them away. Operation Write a Book at Age Twelve was a short-lived experience, but I vowed to return to it once I had a better plan of attack!

Writing has always been a favorite pastime. It relaxes me and is a way of expressing my feelings in a tangible way. In my formative years, I spent many hours writing poems and letters to Jesus. My stomach would fill up with butterflies as the words gushed onto the paper in front of me. Each letter was dressed with colorful drawings to brighten the background, and the pages were carefully stapled together. I was always so proud to share my love for Jesus with my family and remember my mom gently tucking them in between the pages of her special Bible. God deserves my best, and my best was expressed through my writing!

AM I?

Giving God your best doesn't always come naturally. When I was twelve, I know I wasn't aware of spiritual gifts and the promise that God has blessed all of us with at least one of them. However, by the time I had declared my major of communication in college and had secured my first job as a television news anchor, I knew He had writing, producing, and speaking planned for my life. I was still on fire for God, but looking back, it was more on my terms than I was aware.

My first year working in the business world was an eye-opener on many levels. A CBS affiliate hired me upon college graduation to anchor the weekday morning news. I was ecstatic to have a job, let alone be filling an anchor seat with no professional experience whatsoever! It was a whirlwind of finding a place to live, moving my stuff from campus to the apartment, rolling up my sleeves, and getting to work fresh and ready for the day.

Fresh is an understatement for what turned out to be a strict schedule that made me feel anything but fresh or bright eyed! I would liken my schedule to a hamster tirelessly jogging round and round its pinwheel.

My day started at 12:30 a.m. with hot rollers for my hair and heavy camera makeup. It ended at 2:00 p.m. after producing, editing video, anchoring the morning news hour, and delivering four newscasts for a local radio station peppered in between producing and anchoring several cut-ins that aired during the two-hour national news block and producing the noon newscast. I would go home hungry and exhausted every day! It didn't help that the seasoned reporters resented me being there because they wanted my job, a job that went to some punk kid right out of college!

In between work and more work, I would go to the mall and shop for anchor clothes or knickknacks to decorate my new place. Acquiring stuff was at the top of my list.

I was so busy buying and working that there was no time for devotions or finding a church. To this day, I couldn't tell you where the nearest church to my apartment was located. Worshiping God was not a priority;

however, my prayer life was still in tact. Jesus never left my thoughts; I just didn't know how to have an *intimate* relationship with Him, and in the commotion of starting a career, He got put on a shelf.

My lack of sleep led to napping in the afternoon, and my young career soon consumed my every breath. I found myself asking the self-pitying question: is this it?

We all have or will ask this question at some point in our lifetime. It is an inherent part of the human nature to ask, "Is this all life has to offer?" This question also brings us back to that other nagging question of why. "Why do I feel this way?" or "Why am I back at this same point in my life?"

Consider pondering this thought for a moment: Jesus has gone to the depths of the earth to redeem you and me with His blood. He is that secret place you can go to in perfect peace and pray. He is always near, He knows your thoughts and desires, and He wants to have a loving relationship with you. Jesus is the womb of life.

In an Old Testament psalm, we learn that David was knit together in his mother's womb by God. In the New Testament, let's refer back to Romans 6 and read further down in the chapter to verses 19–23. You may have already memorized the last verse, but it's important to read the material that leads up to our memorable favorites to get the whole picture:

> I put this in human terms because you are weak in your natural selves. Just as you used to offer the parts of your body in slavery to impurity and

to ever-increasing wickedness, so now offer them in slavery to righteousness leading to holiness. When you were slaves to sin, you were free from the control of righteousness. What benefit did you reap at that time from the things you are now ashamed of? Those things result in death! But now that you have been set free from sin and have become slaves to God, the benefit you reap leads to holiness, and the result is eternal life. For the wages of sin is death, but the gift of God is eternal life in Christ Jesus our Lord.

Did you notice that all those years ago, Paul asked the same question about whether or not this is it? Look at his response. Living *in* sin leads to death, and being set free *from* sin through Christ leads to eternal life! You can rest in the Lord and know that when you answer to Him, He will answer you back with holiness that leads to a fulfilling life now and forever.

STUDY QUESTIONS

1. List at least one item you can praise God for each day.

2. According to Colossians 2:13–17, what was nailed to the cross with Christ?

3. Define grace.

4. What are you acquiring?

5. List your current top five priorities:

6. Is spending time in the Word anywhere on your list?

7. When have you asked yourself, "Is this it?"

8. True or false: Righteousness = Truth = Christ = eternal life.

9. How did the Apostle Paul answer the "Is this it" question?

THE KINGDOM OF ME

The Bible is filled with stories of great kingdoms that have since come and gone. One of my favorite teachings is in Daniel 5 when we read about the late king of Babylon Nebuchadnezzar's son and heir to the throne, King Belshazzar.

Most of you will agree that you've either heard or used the phrase *the writing is on the wall* to dramatize a point. But did you know that the original usage of that phrase comes from scripture in the Old Testament? In verses 1–4, we learn that Belshazzar is a blasphemous drunk, and in the midst of a banquet with thousands of his nobles, wives, and concubines, he orders his servants to serve wine with the gold and silver goblets taken by Nebuchadnezzar from the temple of God in Jerusalem.

First of all, don't steal from God. Second, don't worship other gods or idols. The Ten Commandments are

God's gift of boundaries to guide us away from sin, sin that Belshazzar was all too willing to gamble his life.

In verse 5, we learn where that chilling phrase comes from: "Suddenly the fingers of a human hand appeared and wrote on the plaster of the wall, near the lampstand in the royal palace. The king watched the hand as it wrote."

The Aramaic inscription in verse 25 is in all capital letters: "*MENE, MENE, TEKEL, PARSIN*," and only Daniel can decipher the message. Daniel tells a trembling Belshazzar in verse 26, "This is what these words mean: Mene: God has numbered the days of your reign and brought it to an end. Tekel: You have been weighed on the scales and found wanting. Peres: Your kingdom is divided and given to the Medes and Persians."

That night, Belshazzar was killed, and his kingdom was handed over to a Mede just as the graffitist fingers foretold.

While I like the dramatics of this message, I can't help but think that I'm different. There are no kings or kingdoms in America, and the closest modern-day fairy tale of one occurred in 1981 when Diana became the Princess of Wales! Unfortunately, I'm wrong again, and this time the ancient fingers of that hand in the book of Daniel are pointing at me.

There were a lot of good times in my short television career. For example, not only was I making 21,000 dollars a year, I was also given a hair and clothing stipend. Chuckle at the low salary, yes, but who can raise his or her hand and say that he or she had any sort of perks in his or her first job? I was thrilled and quickly became friends with my new hairdresser, who gave me a standing monthly appointment.

We would talk about our dreams and aspirations. She had just started her family and was saving to buy a house with her husband. I would talk about the challenges at work and share details of who I was dating at the time. Sometimes I would go on daytrips with a co-worker or out to lunch with the weather guy after the show, and if there was one thing I learned after that first day on the job, it was always go out in public with full makeup and a snazzy coif!

You wouldn't believe how many people recognize you after appearing on television! Most days, I like to throw my hair back into a ponytail with no makeup and put on a pair of jeans with a pullover, but not when you're a local celebrity! No, you're forced to think out every last detail right down to your wardrobe because if you don't, you'll hear about it. It's more like loud whispering that you hear going on behind your back. I kid you not; sometimes I could smell their breath as curious bystanders at the grocery store discussed how I did or didn't look like the person on television. Comments ranged from "Maybe that isn't her" to my personal favorite, "I thought she was taller!"

To me, I was not a celebrity but rather a seriously plain, young woman making a go of her first job in the real world. The glitz and the glam just happened to be a part of the job. Before I knew it, all eyes were on me and where my career was headed after such a hot start.

My college friends made the drive north to catch up on old times. Each family member made a special trip in order to get the grand tour and watch me perform.

The party ended almost as quickly as it started. Just months into my new career, I received notice that I was being terminated. During that same time, I was being stalked and was concerned for my safety. Talk about all shades of stress! Going into detail is still painful. One memory I can share is a verse my sister Shelly wrote onto a sticky note. It was Philippians 4:13: "I can do everything through him who gives me strength." She posted it on my bathroom mirror. To this day, that verse makes me cry because of Christ's tremendous promise of power and strength. I needed to be assured of His promise then and depend upon it now.

Losing my job was a huge disappointment. I can honestly say that my ego wasn't crushed as much as my heart. I truly thought God put me in television because He had a mission.

Over the next several months, I feverishly pursued employment as either a news anchor or reporter. I submitted resume tapes to every station in the country, including Hawaii and Alaska!

To get a job in television, you're required to send in a video of your best work along with a paper resume that lists relevant experience and references. The only problem is that I had limited tapes to send out because I no longer had access to the editing bays at my former job! You can imagine my frustration.

The devil took my vulnerability and fed me with all kinds of lies. I was allowing Satan to talk me into building a kingdom unto myself and I didn't even know it. Finding employment was my main focus, I was seriously distracted, and the devil had a stronghold on my every move. A modern-day kingdom had arisen out of me. Self became the center of my attention.

While I was in between jobs, I lived with my sister Stacey and brother-in-law in Little Rock, Arkansas.

Every other week, my sister would drive me downtown to the nearest unemployment office and wait while I stood in line. I was scared and felt empty. I think she was too, but she encouraged me every step of the way. At one point, we started getting up early to work out together and chose a verse from the Bible to start the day. Trials have a way of turning your attention on to God, and we talked a lot about what it should look like to have a personal relationship with Him.

We both loved Jesus but were struggling about how to get deeper into the Word. Maybe inadequate is a better term for our lack of understanding. I go back to all of the rules us girls were raised with and the impact they had on our every decision. There was no room for mistakes, and expectations were always high. Most of the time, they were too high, and we lived in more fear of stepping out of line than we did in growing in the love of Christ. I believe the term is legalism and is the very man-made laws Jesus disproved and condemned while the Pharisees and Sadducees were plotting His crucifixion.

I find myself praising God not only for the incredible saving grace of Jesus but also for never giving up on any of us! His love never ceases, and He is always in pursuit of blessing us with that love, His plan and purpose for our lives. As you can gather, I was still in search mode and continued to chase after my dreams.

My welcome in Arkansas was starting to wear thin as the days turned into nine months. Finally, by the summer of 1993, I had taken two jobs that brought me back to Michigan. The first was a part-time position at a radio station, and I also lined up a weekend television gig as an associate producer at the ABC affiliate.

I promised myself and others that I would quit whichever job didn't offer full-time employment while secretly praying that God had television for me again. I'm not sure why TV was so important because it caused me nothing but grief. Part of it was the adrenaline rush of meeting daily deadlines. But, to be completely honest, I wanted reassurance that I didn't fail the first time out because of anything I had done wrong.

I was a young, single woman trying to make a living and was making a go of it all by *myself!* Yes, I spent many hours in prayer and I believed in the Bible, Jesus, and His saving grace. Although I claimed to love Jesus, I truly didn't know how to depend on Him for *all* things.

Within three months of working at the radio station, I was offered full time with benefits—an answer to prayer and a huge praise! However, self reared its ugly little head, and before I knew it, I was working over eighty hours a week between both jobs. I made myself believe that God had a full-time television career waiting in the wings, so I held onto my weekend position for dear life.

Control is another word for Satan; I'm convinced of it. Control is bondage—bondage to whatever is number one in your life at any given moment. This form of idolatry is called sin, and the opposite behavior is surrender. Surrender makes room for Jesus and is one ingredient of having a healthy, personal relationship with Him. Putting it more plainly, the devil uses against us our desire to control things. It becomes an open invitation to divert our focus away from God and onto our circumstances. It also breaks our fellowship with God by consuming all of our time. I hadn't figured that out yet; therefore control seemed to have control of me!

Writing this chapter hurts! Rewinding the tape to that time in my life, I can clearly see that I was feeling trapped and alone. I can almost feel those same anxieties as I rationalized I was being a good steward by working two jobs to gain as much professional experience in as little time as possible. I was utilizing my degree and taking responsibility! But if you look in the background of those tapes really close, you will see one spiritually empty young lady.

I'm ashamed to say that from the time I accepted Jesus into my heart when I was seven years old to the time I landed my first couple of jobs, I had not grown in Christ one single bit! I desired a relationship but still didn't know how. Adding fuel to the fire, the long work hours were taking a toll on me physically, and I was emotionally exhausted again.

God will do anything to get your attention, and He used the birth of my niece to get mine! That's the beauty of our great Savior: He uses our current circumstances to draw us near.

For nearly three years I held onto my weekend associate producer job at the local television station. I would go in at eight in the morning and wouldn't get home until eight at night. I was miserable but convinced myself that busy was good! Like before, I was not involved with a church; however, this time I had at least attended a few in my neighborhood and felt good about searching them out on my own. One bright spot to share is that my parents had taught me to seek a church that shared the Gospel and plan of salvation each week, but I remained noncommittal. If there is one thing about my character, it's that I am a creature of habit. Work was the center of my universe, and I put my all into it! I was never late, and I was always available for overtime.

One day, my oldest sister called to share the good news about her pregnancy. I was so excited about becoming an aunt and would call her regularly to get a baby update and even made flight arrangements around the due date so I could celebrate the birth of my sweet niece! The morning I was supposed to fly out, I overslept and missed my flight. My alarm went off, and I never heard a peep. I spent the rest of the day calling around trying to make alternate plans and didn't get to my sister's house until later that evening. I was upset, frazzled, and had inconvenienced my family.

Kelly Grace was born with all of her toes and fingers and was the most beautiful baby I had ever seen. She also slept a lot, but not as much as me. It wasn't enough that I missed my flight, thus shortening my visit by half a day; I spent the rest of the week in bed sleeping. I could barely wake up to eat or help my sister take care of her newborn.

Something had to give, and it had to be me. I was self-destructing. God was knocking at my door to come in, and I kept looking *within myself* to keep things going. I was living my will, not God's. I had gambled His day of rest for a meaningless job that I coveted, and it wasn't working for me at all!

During my return flight I remember being overwhelmed by questions like "How can God use me if I'm always so busy?" Then it dawned on me. I was holding onto something I thought I had to have instead of allowing God to bless me with what He had to give. What I wanted was beating me into submission while Jesus was on the shelf right where I put Him when I first started my career.

Can you relate to what I mean by all of this? Have you been here before? Are you at this point right now? No more excuses! Life had become about me, myself, and I. Sabrina was me-centered, and Christ was nowhere to be found outside of my daily prayers. I had no idea how to have a loving relationship with my Savior, and I was on a spiritual death row.

When I claimed to be different from Belshazzar, I was lying to myself and others. My sin was no different from his in that I idolized my job and worshiped its demanding schedule. Although I didn't blaspheme the Lord in a drunken stupor, I had chosen to put God in a box along with my other forgotten treasures. All of a sudden, like Belshazzar, I could feel my legs tremble as those crusty, ancient fingers began writing on my heart. Surrender each day, trust, and obey.

Is the writing on the wall for you too?

STUDY QUESTIONS

1. Where does the phrase "the writing is on the wall" originate?

2. Who or what is at the *center* of your attention?

3. How have you tried and failed to get up close and personal with God?

4. What rules or past sin(s) are holding you back from growing in the love of Christ?

5. Does fear motivate the decisions you make or do you go to Christ first?

6. Do you believe you can depend on Christ for *all* things?

7. True or false: Control = sin = bondage = Satan.

8. Referring back to your current top five priorities (review Who I Am), give an overview of the first one on your list.

9. Is God trying to get your attention? If so, how?

10. Human or sin nature dictates that we look within ourselves for all the answers. What idols are keeping you from putting Christ first?

11. What do you have to have that is worth forfeiting what God has to give?

12. Is the writing on the wall regarding your spiritual life?

13. What do you think the ancient fingers of Daniel would write on your heart today?

14. Do you struggle with how God would truly love you? Explain why or why not.

SHELF THE SELF

Upon return from celebrating the birth of my niece in Virginia, I quit my weekend job at the local television station. My out-of-control, workaholic behavior was starting to come to light, and I knew I had to give something up in order to make room for Christ. It was time to take God off my bookshelf and put self in its place.

At this point, I had been in morning radio for three years. My role was to add color commentary to the show and deliver headlines and entertainment news. It's typical for the female to fill this position during morning drive, five o'clock to ten o'clock. Generally, you don't hear a female take the lead role unless she's solo in the studio during middays (typically, ten o'clock to two o'clock) or evening drive, which is the time most people are heading home from work, two o'clock to seven o'clock. My position was unique because, at the time, I was working for a locally owned radio group and was expected to switch between two morning shows, plus handle marketing for one of them. Again, I found myself working major hours for little pay.

But here's how God works: Once I quit television, I realized that this is where He had me all along! Radio gave me the platform to share more of my personality with the listening audience than I had ever been able to achieve during my scripted television days. Seventy-five percent of what I said was off-the-cuff, so to speak, and the rest was from my scribbled notes for headlines and entertainment news. Surprising to me were the growing amount of listeners who started reaching out and asking for personal advice because they felt like they knew me from hearing me talk every morning and valued my opinion. What a ministry opportunity—something I completely overlooked because I was previously too busy setting and reaching my own goals.

Leaving television brought my eighty-hour-a-week schedule down to approximately sixty hours; however, my obedience led to an unexpected deliverance! By spring of 1996, I was asked to exclusively work at the Top 40 radio station. Ratings were going up, and the president of the company claimed I was becoming the number one female talent in the market. That move really helped brand me as an identifiable personality in the marketplace. Branding sounds strange because you generally associate it with livestock or in the business world when marketing a new product, but in radio and television, each personality requires the same kind of name recognition. When I was spread so thin over the airwaves of two morning shows, it was virtually impossible for people to correctly identify the station in which I worked.

A second blessing happened when the Federal Communications Commission performed an audit of operations and threatened to fine the owner of the radio group for asking too much of each employee. As a result, a vice president and marketing director were hired to better manage all three stations in the building. Thankfully, I was then only required to co-host one morning show and assist with promotions directly connected to the Top 40 station.

Just as my overall schedule was starting to come together, things were rapidly falling apart in the studio with my co-host. Every morning I would repeat Philippians 4:13 before heading into work because I felt sick to my stomach. As soon as I was asked to put all of my talent into the Top 40 station, my co-host, who doubled as the program director, did everything in his power to humiliate me while we were on the air. If there's one thing I know about sin, it's ugly and comes to life in those who allow their insecurities, anger, and bitterness to infringe upon those around them.

A program director manages all the talent, music, and promotions of the radio station. In larger markets, like Detroit or Los Angeles, the program director delegates the daily selection of music to a music director who also meets with record representatives from the various labels. Programming a station is a huge responsibility but has its perks, and it's the perks that can lead one astray, as in this case. The more time I spent in the studio instead of in between studios, the more I witnessed this person jeopardizing the license of the station. He also went out of his way to turn off my microphone midsentence or insidiously mock me during the daily live broadcasts. It got so bad that audience members started reporting him to management; all the while, God was preparing me for another big change.

The day I prayed to God that I wasn't able to work at the station any longer is the day I walked into work and was informed that three people had been fired, including my program director/co-host! Firings without cause are frequent in the world of broadcasting, but this time, all three had been found to be conspiring together and were promptly released of their duties.

Have you come close to throwing your arms in the air in despair and given up on God? Despair is another word for hopelessness and can be remedied by putting Christ at the center of your life. I learned another valuable lesson about persevering to the end of a trial, and Zephaniah 3:17 says, "The Lord your God is with you, he is mighty to save. He will take great delight in you, he will quiet you with his love, he will rejoice over you with singing."

When I whimpered in prayer that particular morning, God calmed me with a tender, "Shhh. It's all right, Sabrina. I am right here to take care of you," and then He softly sang a lullaby to me as I was being renewed in His Spirit.

STUDY QUESTIONS

1. Are you willing to give up and walk away from God for good or would you like to learn how to be renewed in His Spirit?

2. Spend each day this week journaling about your past and present circumstances. Scripture teaches that nothing comes to you before going through Him. The day before your group meets, spend intimate time with God and pray for Him to quiet you with His love. If you've never petitioned His love before, simply pray Zephaniah 3:17, plus read from your journal. Listen. What do you hear?

TRADING CENTERS

God sings! And it is His steady voice that helped me get through the next year of perpetual changes at the Top 40 radio station.

The day I learned three people had been let go was the day I learned I was taking the now former program director's room aboard a station-sponsored cruise to the Eastern Caribbean! I had never been on such an exotic vacation and was barely making ends meet with a salary that was thousands less than what I was making at CBS. Leading up to the news of this defaulted trip, I was preparing to hand in my notice and find employment elsewhere. The in-studio ridicule and dishonest, off-the-air activity had become too much to bear. When I said I was whimpering the morning of the firings, I wasn't kidding. It was that bad.

Of course, things started looking up when I scurried home to start packing for this unexpected, all-expenses-paid cruise! I instantly became an expert on how to be a gracious cruise director and prior to the trip attended two briefings to meet with the listeners who had signed up to go with me. I have great memories of that vacation and came home with a really neat group of new friends! God knows when you need a reprieve—time to take a deep breath and hit the reset button—and this was it because the next twelve months radically changed my life again.

Upon my return from the weeklong cruise, I was back on the air with a variety of guests who filled in while management listened to résumé tapes in their search for my new co-host. Over the next three months, I was told they had narrowed the candidates down to three men; they had found a new program director, plus they announced that the station was transferring to another city! Before I only had to work with one person, and now I was going to have a new boss and new co-host in a different part of the state!

If getting up at three in the morning wasn't early enough, I now had to adjust my drive time, which turned out to be an hour more each way. My life seemed like it was upside down again, but this time I knew I was supposed to make the move. I felt God had spared me from being fired along with everyone else because He still had plans for me at the radio station. I even started praying—for as long as He wanted me to have a voice in the market, I would focus on Him and follow His lead. This was the beginning of my spiritual transformation.

By fall of 1996, I had found and settled into a new apartment that was just minutes away from the new studio. My new boss (program director) started a few weeks before my new co-host arrived, so we had the opportunity to bond and get acquainted with each other. Even after my bad experience, I never doubted that the new staff would all get along because I knew God was in control. However, I later learned that my new co-host complained to our boss after our first week on the air together and told him that it wasn't going to work! To which he said, "If you don't make it work, then you're out of a job!" Between the support of the president of the radio station, who had made that clear to the new program director, and my celebrity status in the market, I was secure.

Change perhaps is my middle name because I seem to handle it well. My new boss only stayed with the company for a couple of years before he took a similar position in a larger radio market. The good news is that the chemistry between my co-host and I seemed to be getting better and better with each day, and by now we were laughing at the story about his arrogant diva fit.

We both had a heart for kids and decided to form a nonprofit organization. The intent was to be able to raise large sums of money through corporate donations in order to build safe playgrounds for area school districts or take ill and disadvantaged children on day field trips. Outings ranged from taking a busload of kids to an apple orchard for a hayride, games, and cider and donuts to a horse ranch to learn how to go horseback riding! Those were *good* times.

During this same time period, my co-host and I were being courted by a separate radio group to work for them, but we refused their offers. By 2000, the company decided to purchase our frequency so we would have no choice! For the first time in my radio career, I was going to be working under contract plus have a guaranteed bonus structure for reaching a certain quarterly rating in the market. My salary tripled in the first year and went up from there.

Although we were still performing on the same frequency and format, a new studio had to be built to accommodate us at the new building. Once settled, our ratings started to steadily go up, and we managed to stay in the top five of about thirty or forty stations in the market. My job remained secure.

Up until working for the new radio group, I was handwriting all of my sports, weather, entertainment, and newscasts. It was a huge help when they purchased a laptop for me to use in the studio; plus, Internet access added a whole new dimension to the content of our show!

I've never really been interested in computers and always thought of them as an inconvenient convenience until e-mail. E-mail is responsible for the next step in my transformation and first ministry effort. Most days, I would get about a hundred messages from listeners who either wanted to chat about something I said during the show or to ask my advice. Some of the questions were so personal that I decided to have a Web site developed so I could communicate to each listener at a secure address. I also didn't want the company to be held liable for anything I advised. Pretty soon, I was meeting up for coffee with two or three people a week to either encourage or help them get back on their feet.

All along, God had this ministry for me. He knows I have a heart for one-on-one meetings and used that passion to give me a platform to spread the good news about Jesus. Do you know that in the nearly eight years that I was able to grow the ministry that not one person complained to my employer or tried to sue me? God's will was being done, and He protected me from all of those concerns—more divine security.

For as long as I was with the new radio group, management seemed to always be courting our morning team (my co-host and I) to switch formats. The company owned seven radio frequencies in our market alone, and the idea was to build the same ratings at some of their lesser performing stations so they could make more money. Again, we resisted until winter of 2005.

There were pros and cons to making the move, including concerns of heading into low ratings at the new frequency, inheriting a new demographic, which would require drastic content changes, and the challenge of building a new listening base. My main concern was my ministry and leaving listeners I had come to love, but the move came with a promise that the new station's signal was more powerful and therefore would reach a larger region of listeners. Again, I felt God was leading me to make the move, which put us in front of yet another program director.

I had come to learn in my then twelve years in radio that people come and go, especially on-air talent and program directors. Within months of starting at the new frequency, we were greeted by a new leader who helped take the station to number one in two ratings books. Bonus!

The more money I earned, the more it was used to help others. Every day, my eyes were opened to see the hurts and needs of the people in our listening audience. There were even needs within the confines of the radio group, and I was able to reach out to a few people and offer encouragement. My motto was and is today, "Everyone is hurting about something this morning," and I felt it was my job to at least put a smile on their face. Humor has a way of getting your mind off of the day-to-day struggles. The sillier the banter got between me and my co-host, the more listeners would call-in, and then we would all laugh together!

Times were about to change again, but God was faithfully preparing my heart for it. At the new frequency, I had the awesome opportunity to host a weekend contemporary Christian music hour with a television friend of mine. Prior to this gig, we unsuccessfully tried to get a separate program underwritten that targeted teens and parents. It was fun to finally be able to work together.

On top of my morning and weekend show commitments, I was using my spare time to create programming for syndication. It was rather comprehensive, so I invited five people to become my partners. My intention was to develop and host programming suitable for broadcast via satellite radio or through either one of three radio syndication companies. Most likely, I would have to make a choice between morning radio and national syndication if someone were to pick up my show, but at this point I wasn't clear whether this was God's will or my own. All I knew was that syndication had always been a professional goal of mine, and the timing seemed right. According to my contract, however, I needed corporate permission to pursue my endeavor. But guess what? This time it wasn't the program director who was let go, but the general manager, which brought everything to a screeching halt. I reluctantly put the project on hold until I could secure a meeting with the new guy and try to get his approval.

On the outside it appeared that life was moving along nicely, and truthfully nothing was glaringly wrong. My heart was simply changing, and it was God who was prompting the change. My goals were centering more and more on how many people I could reach and how to share Christ with each of them.

Meanwhile, my bunk bed buddy was able to make her annual trip to my house, and she asked if she could join my co-host and me in the studio each morning. Of course, the answer was yes. She had become friends with my co-host, whom I now considered more like a brother than a co-worker. By the second or third day, she decided not to come in anymore and told me that something was different about him. I agreed.

A lot had been going on behind the scenes, including the new general manager coming on board. Folks seemed to be on their best behavior and privately concerned for their jobs. I trusted the Lord and seemed to be the rare exception. At this crucial time of change at the radio station, my sister informed me that she didn't see me working there anymore and advised me to get on my knees in prayer. God has consistently used my bunk bed buddy to get my focus back on Him. She was rather insistent that He was preparing me for something else, and as I explained earlier, I was already at a pivotal point in my career with a growing passion for a syndication deal.

When I finally got an appointment with the new general manager to ask for permission to proceed with my project, he turned me down flat and said the only green light I had was to continue putting my energy into my performance on the morning show! Clearly, I had to honor his decision or quit my job.

My sister and I prayed together, and I prayed alone. My main petition was that it would be hard for me to personally walk away from such a great job but that I would be obedient to go wherever God had prepared a place. This was all coming together at a time when the greed on Wall Street had taken half of my retirement investments and the state of Michigan was already ranked forty-ninth in the country for the highest rate of unemployment! I also prayed for the heartache of walking away from my Web site ministry, nonprofit children's charity, and weekend contemporary Christian hour. However, this time I can joyfully claim that Christ was at the center of my every thought, action, and prayer. He was not on a shelf but by my side.

Three weeks to the day that my sister notified me that she was sure God had something else for my life, I was let go after fourteen years on the air. I had the same job over two stations and with two different companies. I answered to countless program directors and general managers who had come and gone over the years, and now it was my turn. As I was being led upstairs to the human resources department, I looked up and praised God for answering my prayer according to His will. Although I didn't expect to lose my job, I didn't expect to keep it either. What I did hope for was complete peace, and He granted it on the spot! The human resources director even asked how I could be so peaceful, giving me the opportunity to witness to one last person before being escorted out of the building.

My co-host of eleven years was the designated person to escort me to my car. I'll never forget the look on his face when I walked out of and back into the studio. All he said was, "I feel like Judas."

During the walk from the studio to my car, I learned why. He informed me that he had secretly negotiated a contract for a position at a different station within the building, received a raise, and that this particular format was a dream come true for him. I can only speak for myself and say that yes, I was deeply hurt by what I was hearing, but I was also silently praising God—

this time for allowing me to trade centering on self to Christ. My focus was on Christ, not my circumstances. I was covered with an indescribable peace and granted instant grace to lovingly say good-bye and offer forgiveness to my now former co-host.

Where would I be without my Savior?

STUDY QUESTIONS

1. Describe a time of struggle and strain in your life.

2. Has God ever answered your prayer in the last hour? What was the outcome?

3. At what point has your walk with God shown evidence of spiritual growth?

4. Is there a difference between success and God's blessing?

5. What is the ministry God has planned for you?

6. Has God ever prompted a change of heart in your career goals, family, or other area of your life?

7. Are you more prone to worry or trust God when times get tough?

8. What is your source for peace?

9. Is it possible to have peace outside of God?

10. Do you know the peace, joy, and contentment Christ promises in the midst of all circumstances?

*Pause here to encourage group to take the online spiritual gifts test. Answers will aid understanding in the chapter "3D." (http://www.TeamMinistry.com)

PART TWO

3D

Grab your 3-D glasses. We're goin' to the movies! Oh, and don't forget to get the big tub o' popcorn smothered in butter because this is an epic! "In the beginning God created the heavens and the earth" (Genesis 1:1). Wow, Moses could give us all lessons on how to start a powerful script! Coming up with that first sentence always takes the most time, and it helps when God is revealing His Word through you! Second hardest is figuring out how to bring everything together for a happy ending. In this chapter, I am going to touch on God's character through the very Word He breathed (2 Timothy 3:16). So, put on those 3-D glasses and keep 'em on until the conclusion of this epic. Not only will they help us focus, but they will also reveal His likeness before our very own eyes.

First, let's discuss how to become a part of the body of Christ. When I get together with my bunk bed buddy sister, Stacey, I spend time with her friends and vice versa when she's in town visiting me. It's become tradition that each friend either meets us for coffee or we spend the day at one another's homes to catch up on the happenings we missed in between trips. I've come to really look forward to these outings because it's like finding that favorite, old sweater stuffed in the back of your closet when winter rolls around—comforting and warm.

One particularly frosty Christmas, we were all snug at a friend's house when we got on the subject of spiritual gifts. Three cups of coffee into the conversation, it was agreed that discernment was on my list. What a compliment, I thought, but the truth is that *all* spiritual gifts are super special, and we *all* have them! God didn't just choose a few. He created us *all* for His glory and with great design.

Spiritual gifts are outlined four times in scripture, and one is earmarked especially for you! Some of us have more than one; however, none of us can claim them all. It would defeat the purpose of the body of Christ coming together through each one of us. One believer depends on the other to serve the Lord!

Seven gifts are found in Romans 12:6–8 and include serving, teaching, encouragement, giving, leadership, showing mercy, and prophecy. There are eighteen in all that fall into one of three categories, including miraculous, enabling, or team gifts. If you didn't already know this, Paul was spiritually gifted with many that fell into the miraculous category, including tongues. He goes into great detail of what that means in his first letter to the Corinthian church by sharing the blessings or loss it can bring to the body. What struck me the most is how cautious he is in describing the limitless power of this particular gift of the Holy Spirit:

> For anyone who speaks in a tongue does not speak to men but to God. Indeed, no one understands him; he utters mysteries with his spirit. But everyone who prophesies speaks to men for their strengthening, encouragement and comfort. He who speaks in a tongue edifies himself, but he who prophesies edifies the church.
>
> 1 Corinthians 14:2–4

There's a distinction and that is that anyone of us has the free will to either use our spiritual gifts to help ourselves (self) or build the body (the church; Christ is the head). Speaking in a tongue that no one understands except for you and God only benefits the speaker. Prophesying is the gift of revealing God's Truth to other believers who are busy using their spiritual gifts to also serve.

Additional gifts are mentioned in 1 Corinthians 12, Ephesians 4, and 1 Peter 4. In the back of this book, you will find a link in my notes that offers an online test that will help you learn more about where God is leading you to serve within the body of His church (Gilbert 2009).

Speaking of the body of Christ, is it possible to truly experience God? If you're like me, things start to click when you can thoroughly examine what you're trying to understand. There's something about the tangible that brings the big picture into focus; however, there is great danger in approaching God in this manner. In the second commandment, God forbids us to make an idol in His image (Exodus 20:4–6). What that means is that we all try at some point to get our minds around God, and we go to great lengths to bring Him to our spiritual level of understanding. We often want to contain God so we can manage our relationship with Him. In this shrinking process, we miss who our provider of infinite resources is and sometimes end up worshiping a man-made, finite god.

Have you ever wondered why we have so many senses? I mean, hearing is cool, but why are we made to taste, feel, smell, and see? If God has never been seen by anyone, then what's the point? You're shaking your head at me, and I know that seeing is a huge blessing when it comes to avoiding blunt objects in our paths, but seriously, if our eyes are supposed to be on Him and we can't see Him, then why did God give us sight? Since we're on a roll here, how about the sense of touch? I mean, come on. I can no more reach out and grab Jesus' robe than you can. If there's one of our present-day senses that could possibly be salvageable in our relationship with Christ, it would be our ability to hear Him answering our prayers. The other senses seem to be a waste.

I've just explained a pretty pathetic scene after stating that God is 3D! And I find myself wavering between emotions rather than sticking to the proof in

Scripture that God is three in one. He is my Father, He is the Son, He is the Spirit, and He's blessed me with five distinct senses that I may use to experience the fullness of His awesome glory. For example, listen to how God responded to Moses when he expressed doubt about having the right tools to lead the Israelites out of Egypt: "The Lord said to him, 'Who gave man his mouth? Who makes him deaf or mute? Who gives him sight or makes him blind? Is it not I, the Lord? Now go; I will help you speak and will teach you what to say'" (Exodus 4:11–12).

What a load of promises, and if you continue to observe the life of Moses, after he faithfully agrees to trust in the Lord, each one of the tools God promised were in fact bestowed upon him at the right place and time. First, Moses had to make a choice just like you and I must. We might ask the question: Do I believe in a 3-D God whom I cannot see, touch, smell, taste, or hear? Moses actually had several conversations with God, including at the burning bush; however, we have never heard His voice. Or have we? Yes is the answer, and Job tells us how! In chapter 33:14–15 he said, "For God does speak—now one way, now another—though man may not perceive it. In a dream, in a vision of the night, when deep sleep falls on men as they slumber in their beds." So even while we're sleeping and unaware of His presence, the Lord is talking to us.

God has spoken to me a time or two. More recently it happened while I was brushing my teeth! It's a good thing to know that God really means it when He says in Luke 18:22, " … come [as you are], follow me" (words in brackets are mine) because I was a little embarrassed that He didn't wait until my breath was a little fresher.

Losing my morning radio job of fourteen years allowed me to continue developing programming for syndication with my five partners. Over the next ten months, I developed and presented the material to heads of syndication companies as well as potential national sponsors. While all six of us were getting close to signing a partner agreement, I was silently praying for clarity about how to handle something that was said during a past meeting. It happened while I was asking each partner to make an additional financial investment in order to head into the new year debt-free. I had made the comment that God would honor our good stewardship, to which one of the partners quipped, "What does God have to do with running a business?" Mind you, this person openly stated that he and his family were churchgoers and in a past meeting voted in favor of tithing ten percent of any future company earnings. I was stunned.

God laid that statement on my heart because He had other plans for my life. For ten days I prayed for guidance when God said, "Don't be fearful for what's to come." *Uh-oh!* I thought and quickly wiped the foam off my mouth while rushing to the phone to call my sister so we could speculate what that could possibly mean. Do you know what she said? "How awesome! God hasn't ever talked to me!" You may be saying the same thing, but don't feel left out and keep listening for His voice.

In the meantime, look for God's communication in

other ways. For example, before you go to bed at night, ask God to help you with something specific. Promise that you trust in His power and will for your life. You may even ask God to lift the burden from your mind and ask for a good night of rest (Psalm 127:2). Finding information pertaining to the contents of this book allowed me the privilege to specifically pray for guidance in His Word. During devotions one morning, God led me to the precise scripture He wanted me to study and share with you! At first I didn't even recognize that He had answered my prayer until I cross-referenced a verse that popped off the page at me. Believe it or not, I shouted, "Thank you, Jesus!" and got on my knees and praised Him for His provision. Sometimes we just have to ask, seek, or knock, and let Jesus into our daily messes (Matthew 7:7) and then listen for His answer!

I have to say that I've never given much thought to what God may or may not smell like! Kind of weird if you think about it for too long, but now that the question is out there, my interest has piqued! Sure enough, 2 Corinthians 2:15–16 says, "For we are to God the aroma of Christ among those who are being saved and those who are perishing. To the one we are the smell of death; to the other, the fragrance of life. And who is equal to such a task?" My Application Study Bible is great for giving historical details, and I highly recommend it if you're looking for an additional resource (Life Application Study Bible, NIV).

Around AD 55–57, the Apostle Paul wrote the church

in Corinth to warn them against false teachers during the intense rule of the Roman Empire. Tradition has it that after winning a battle, the Roman general would burn incense to the gods and parade his new treasures in front of his captives. The aroma was sweet to the winners and the smell of death to the losers. Paul reveals that the *fragrance of life* is God. When we spread the gospel, we are in His midst with the pleasing aroma of His presence. In turn, we are *the aroma of Christ* whose Spirit is in those of us who have accepted Him as Savior! Isn't this amazing stuff? Before I stumbled upon this verse, I had some fun listing all of the things I imagined Christ could have smelled like. For sure He smelled sweet like nard (the perfume used by Mary of Bethany to wash His feet), ripe like a vine of grapes ready for harvest (we smell like branches!), or bittersweet like the wine vinegar soaked sponge lifted to Jesus' lips before He spoke His final words, "It is finished" (John 19:30).

A third sense is feeling and is rather complex in that we can sense someone's presence without seeing, feel an emotion, physically feel and even feel or check out a situation. The main definition of feel is "To perceive through the sense of touch." (The American Heritage Dictionary of the English Language, third edition n.d.)

God can touch our hearts through the Holy Spirit (1 Samuel 10:26), Jesus physically touched his disciples and the sick touched Him to be healed (Matthew 14:36;

17:7), and in Zechariah 2:8 we learn "For this is what the Lord Almighty says: 'After he has honored me and has sent me against the nations that have plundered you—for whoever touches you touches the apple of his eye.'" God touches us emotionally and spiritually while Jesus physically came in contact with Creation; plus, He uses others to touch our lives.

My five-year-old nephew, Storm, is a perfect example of how God uses others to touch your heart. What a guy! Between you and me, I call him my little *froggie* because he looks like one when he takes his bath at night. He loves the water and jumps from one end of the tub to the other until the skin on his fingers are all shriveled up like raisins. Not a bath goes by without him belting out some sort of song or telling a story with his bath toys; it's an absolute joy to hear and watch him play. Since he loves music so much, we started a tradition of playing old records on my antique Victrola when he's at my house, and we laugh and dance until bedtime. One night, he put his hand in mine and asked if he could choose the music before gently flopping in my lap to take a look-see at the records. Crocodile tears began rolling down my cheeks as I was sure this was how children flocked to be with Jesus. There's something about touch and how God blesses us with His Spirit when we desire His presence most.

We may be 20/20 by the time we get through all the ways we personally get to know our Lord and Savior! Speaking of sight, this is the toughest sense to experience because Scripture tells us that no one has ever seen God (John 1:18), probably because His Glory is so bright that if you looked directly at His Light, you would get burnt to a crisp. We know this after reading Exodus 33:18–22:

> Then Moses said, "Now show me your glory." And the Lord said, "I will cause all my goodness to pass in front of you, and I will proclaim my name, the Lord, in your presence. I will have mercy on whom I will have mercy, and I will have compassion on whom I will have compassion. But," he said, "you cannot see my face, for no one may see me and live." Then the Lord said, "There is a place near me where you may stand on a rock. When my glory passes by, I will put you in a cleft in the rock and cover you with my hand until I have passed by. Then I will remove my hand and you will see my back; but my face must not be seen."

Can you imagine? No one except Jesus, who is in the image of God, has seen God. The Apostle John, who lived with Jesus, tells us, "The Word became flesh and made his dwelling among us. We have seen his glory, the glory of the One and Only, who came from the Father, full of grace and truth" (John 1:14). Jesus shares a parable about spiritual blindness in John 9:37 and reveals that anyone who has seen Him has also seen the Son of Man. Later, He confirms that He and the Father are one (John 10:30). Perhaps the best verse of all is in John 14 when Jesus rebukes Philip by answering him, "Anyone who has seen me has seen the Father. How can you say, 'Show us the Father'" (verse 9)?

We see God every day! He's in our front lawn, in the clouds, and quite honestly He looks back at us in the mirror because we were made in His image (Genesis 1:26–27)! Jesus is the only One who can claim to have literally seen God (John 6:46). It is true that Adam and Eve *heard* God walking in the garden of Eden, but Scripture never says that they *saw* Him. What's even more interesting is that they could see, but their eyes were not opened until they ate from the tree of the knowledge of good and evil. Once their eyes were opened, then they became wise to their nakedness and covered themselves with fig leaves:

> Then the man and his wife heard the sound of the Lord God as he was walking in the garden in the cool of the day, and they hid from the Lord God among the trees of the garden. But the Lord God called to the man, "Where are you?" He answered, "I heard you in the garden, and I was afraid because I was naked; so I hid."
>
> Genesis 3:8–10

Ever since then, we have been separated from Him; however, "nothing in all creation is hidden from God's sight. Everything is uncovered and laid bare before the eyes of him to whom we must give account" (Hebrews 4:13). God knows our thoughts and what is going on in our hearts. Sin is what separates us from Him, and when Christ returns, we will be reunited with God in all His splendor and Glory in heaven. Therefore, "We live by faith, not by sight" (2 Corinthians 5:7).

The fifth and final sense is taste.

During the Last Supper, "Jesus took bread, gave thanks and broke it, and gave it to his disciples, saying, 'Take and eat; this is my body'" (Matthew 26:26). Today, believers eat bread in remembrance of Him during communion. Bread is a symbol of Christ's atoning body.

A second way we taste is through God's Word. When we first profess faith in Christ we are told, "Like newborn babies, crave pure spiritual milk, so that by it you may grow up in your salvation, now that you have tasted that the Lord is good" (1 Peter 2:2–3).

When Jesus walked the earth, He offered mankind what is called the Bread of Life. Jesus performed many great miracles that either improved or prolonged peoples' lives; however, His divine purpose was and is to offer eternal life to *all*. Jesus promises, "For the bread of God is he who comes down from heaven and gives life to the world" (John 6:33), and later declares, "I am the bread of life. He who comes to me will never go hungry, and he who believes in me will never be thirsty" (John 6:35).

Ingest Psalm 119:103 each time you open your Bible and pray, "How sweet are your *words* to my *taste*, sweeter than honey to my mouth!" (Italics are mine.)

Isn't God awesome? From Genesis to Revelation, we can sense the Lord in all His Glory through Jesus who became the Word in flesh. It is this Word that we can touch, see, hear, smell, and taste in order to experience His fullness.

STUDY QUESTIONS

1. List your spiritual gift(s).

2. Are you guilty of trying to define God?

3. Why or why not do you believe in a 3-D God?

4. Outside of God speaking to His believers, what are some other ways He communicates with us?

5. In 2 Corinthians 2:15–16, Paul says we are *the aroma of Christ* to God. To whom are we the *smell of death?*

6. Share a time God has touched your life.

7. Who has seen God and how do we see Him today?

8. What have or are you trying to conceal from God?

9. How can we utilize our sense of taste in relation to God?

10. What resource is available to all who seek the opportunity to touch, see, taste, smell, and hear God?

I AM

Experiencing God through our five senses is just one part of building a relationship with Him. A second is understanding the trinity: God the Father, the Son, and His Spirit. There is no scripture that mentions the trinity, but plenty that detail three persons in One. My personal favorite is found in Matthew 28 when Jesus commanded his disciples, "Therefore go and make disciples of all nations, baptizing them in the name of the Father and of the Son and of the Holy Spirit" (verse 19).

FATHER

With music always swirling through my mind, I decided one day to put lyrics to a song I kept humming. Mind you, this was several years ago, but it has to do with how God is our Father and He watches over us. Knowing that God is my Heavenly Father, I wanted to note about the role He intended for my biological dad whom He appointed as guardian over us girls. It started as a rhyme until I rearranged the letters of *Father* to spell *heart*. Here are the rest of the lyrics inspired that day:

> Every father is a son.
> You, Lord, are all in one
> Father, Son, and Spirit,
> Redemption to all who believe it.
>
> Holy,
> Everlasting,
> Almighty,
> Righteous One of
> Truth...
>
> Your name is all heart,
> The source of life and light.
> Father, oh, Father
> Leader, protector, and provider.
> You, Lord, are all in one
> My Heart, Spirit, and Son

Since the beginning of time, men have been designated by God to be the head of the household. The father is the heart or main vessel that pumps blood through the rest of the family to keep it alive and well. God is the first Father who created Adam and Eve. Jesus is the last Adam, or Father of all.

When I think of role models, I think of my parents, who were my only example of how to behave and learn how to do the things that required experience or knowledge. Granted, not all parents are good role models, and you may agree that you substituted one or both with another relative or friend. Since God is the first Father and Jesus is the Father of all, let's take a look at the example they set for us. In Genesis, God walked with Adam and Eve in the garden of Eden. He expressed His unconditional love, offered provision, set boundaries, gave them privacy, responsibility (name creatures, etc.), ownership, and companionship. As their Father, God freely gave of all He had so they could celebrate Creation together. God sent Jesus to live among us to refresh us with His promise to do all these things both on earth and in heaven. Both God and Christ desire to share their kingdom with those who trust in His authority and have taught us how to nurture a relationship.

The Apostle Paul describes our legacy with the Father in 1 Corinthians 11:7: "A man ought not to cover his head, since he is the image and glory of God; but the woman is the glory of man." Have you ever considered yourself *of* God, part of His Spirit? This takes us back to the book of Genesis when God created Adam out of the dust of the ground and in His image (2:7) and later Eve from a rib of Adam or man (2:22).

God loves us unconditionally; however, we have been separated from Him ever since Adam and Eve sinned in the garden of Eden. Therefore, He prepared the perfect sacrifice to restore us, His only begotten Son.

SON

A second part of the trinity is Jesus, the Christ (Greek), the Messiah (Hebrew), the Word in flesh. Prophets predicted God would send His Anointed One to live among us to reveal another dimension of His holiness. Jesus' purpose was to teach in love and pay the price for our redemption with His blood.

Jesus is a second chance, not a last resort. He is the only way we are promised to be made blameless before the Father. Second Corinthians 4:6 says, "For God, who said, 'Let light shine out of darkness,' made his light shine in our hearts to give us the light of the knowledge of the glory of God in the face of Christ." (Goodrick and III n.d.)

You may be a little uncomfortable at this point, and I sincerely understand! It's nice to learn about Christ, but knowing how to live for Him is when it starts getting complicated. Well, my friend, you are not alone. It has taken nearly forty years for me to start getting personal with Him, and it's going to take another forty-plus! Being in relation to our Savior is a lifetime commitment. And every time I think I have it all figured out, He gives me a dose of "Oh, no you don't!" and I humbly fall on my knees before Him.

The three dimensions of the trinity are not for us to get our minds around and micromanage. His glory will be revealed to us when Christ returns to claim *all* creation and only then. No, all we need to understand today is that God loves us unconditionally and wants to be in a relationship with us, and He sent His Son to do it. It's that simple-hard.

Simple-hard? Yes! Having a real relationship with our Creator is not easy, but if you seek Him in the Bible, you will find Him everywhere! The simple part is choosing to follow His Way. The hard part is circumventing our human nature to sin. The honest truth of the matter is that the closer you draw to Jesus, the harder Satan will work to divert your attention. That's why Christ left us with His Spirit until He returns (2 Corinthians 5:5).

HOLY SPIRIT

Some would say the proof is in the pudding, but I believe all answers are in the Bible. For instance, Acts 2:32–33 teaches, "God has raised this Jesus to life, and we are all witnesses of the fact. Exalted to the right hand of God, he has received from the Father the promised Holy Spirit and has poured out what you now see and hear."

One day I had what my sister calls a light-bulb moment when I personally experienced the Holy Spirit. My last day as a CBS morning news anchor fell on Christmas Eve day. For three weeks leading up to my termination, I came into work and performed my contractual duties all the while a new person was brought in for me to train to take over my spot! I was hurting on the inside and smiling on the outside. It was important that my future ex-co-workers saw a woman of faith, a person who lives what she said she believes. On my drive home, I would cry until my drive into work the next morning. In three heart-wrenching weeks, I learned a valuable lesson. God had never once left my side and was true to His promise that He would never forsake me (Deuteronomy 31:6) by surrounding me with family who took turns helping me through this tough transition.

What was I thinking? The moment anyone accepts Christ into his or her heart, His Spirit takes over to guide and counsel us in all good things. It will always be my job to either include Him in my daily routine or tidily tuck Him in a corner or closet. Let there be no mistake in understanding that even though I tuck and push Him away, He is still present!

I'm so thankful that He never left my side when I subtly moved in the opposite direction. I desperately needed Him to follow through on his promise in Psalm 121:3–4 that "He will not let your foot slip—he who watches over you will not slumber; indeed, he who watches over Israel will neither slumber nor sleep." I also needed His grace to get through my last day as a news anchor, and I knew I couldn't do it alone. For the grand finale show, I prayed the Holy Spirit would speak my final words. The audience had no idea it was my last day, nor was I able to officially say good-bye. Just before tossing the local portion of the morning show to the network (*The Early Show*), the Spirit prompted me to say happy birthday to Jesus, and my farewell turned into an invitation to celebrate the birth of Christ!

Oodles of viewer faxes and phone calls rolled in for hours after my last show. As I recall, my ex-boss was not a happy camper, probably because none of them were *negative!* Here is one I stumbled upon just before I was escorted out of the building:

Just wanted to compliment Sabrina on her nice manner. Was very impressed with her wishing everyone a Merry Christmas and making the statement about the fact that we should remember what this season is really all about.

K. F. of Traverse City, MI

Glory was brought to His name through the most challenging of circumstances and through someone who had put Him in a tidy little box until she thought she needed His help. Sound familiar?

Time and again, I have been forgiven. From birth until now, I have continually turned my back on His love and called His provision my own. I have professed faith in Christ and stolen His glory whenever the spotlight shone on me. Yet, we are still promised that the Holy Spirit will take over when we are at a loss of words to ask for help:

> In the same way, the Spirit helps us in our weakness. We do not know what we ought to pray for, but the Spirit himself intercedes for us with groans that words cannot express. And he who searches our hearts knows the mind of the Spirit, because the Spirit intercedes for the saints in accordance with God's will.
>
> Romans 8:26–27

I have been so incredibly humbled by this verse. No matter how low I go, the Holy Spirit is there on my behalf to pray for restoration to the Father through Christ.

Are you ready to learn how to take the spiritual baby steps that lead to an amazing, deep, and loving relationship with Christ? This simply hard relationship with our Creator is im*possible,* minus the *im!* You see, the *im* that would normally spell self or *im*possibility in our language is the capital I AM in Hebrew that stands for the unchanging nature of YHWH. God said to Moses, "I AM WHO I AM. This is what you are to say to the Israelites: 'I AM has sent me to you'" (Exodus 3:14).

First things first, you may want to invest in a spiritual toolbox to add five essential principles to get you started. I will briefly share them here and go into more detail in the chapter Faith and the S.T.O.P. Principle.

We've already learned that we are all born into a fallen world and are therefore sinners. God sent His Son to pave the way to redemption and forgiveness of sins by nailing it to the cross. Now you must determine your faith in Christ. Do you believe you are a sinner in need of a Savior? If so, admit your sin and ask Jesus to forgive you and to become the Lord of your life by praying:

> Dear Jesus, I confess that I am a sinner in need of forgiveness and redemption by the blood you shed on the cross at Calvary to pay my sin debt in full. Please have mercy on me and fill me with Your grace and love that I may have eternal life in the name of Jesus. Lord, I want to follow Your will for my life and pray that You fill me with Your Spirit to guide me in all things, Amen.

If you prayed this prayer for the first time, you are forgiven by a risen Lord! He promises when you confess with your mouth, "Jesus is Lord," and believe in your heart that God raised him from the dead, you will be saved (Romans 10:9), and I would be delighted to hear from you so I can encourage you in your new walk with the Lord. My Web site address is located on the back cover of this book. I would also like to hear from anyone who may have more questions before making this life-altering decision. As I said earlier, it is my pleasure to come alongside anyone who is seeking answers and/or encouragement!

After professing faith in Christ, you'll need to add surrender. If you have not made a decision to accept Christ, then the following four tools will not excuse you from answering that question. Faith in Christ is a matter of the condition of your heart, and if you choose to deny Him, you deny God too (1 John 2:22–23).

Surrender is the opposite of control and involves making the personal decision to pick up your cross and trust the Spirit to lead you in all things. Dedicating your life to Jesus means you no longer depend on yourself for all the answers, and surrendering control may mean daily, oftentimes hourly, submission to God's authority.

Countless believers confirm that the closer you get to God, the harder and more often Satan attacks. The more we're attacked, the more tools we need to keep our focus where it belongs! Jesus told his disciples in John 14:1, "Do not let your hearts be troubled. Trust in God;

trust also in me." Trust is a biggie because it's easier said than done and is a close second to surrender.

I struggle in this area every day of my walk! While I think I'm trusting, my human nature steps in and makes a mess of things. What gives? Usually, it's a distraction of some sort, and the devil loves to taunt by showing us what we don't have or tempt us with something the Lord has forbade us to do. Check out how God answers Jeremiah in chapter 12 when he asks, "Why does the way of the wicked prosper" (verse 1)? This is a common question, and God always answers the same way with the promise that He will uproot *all* sin but have mercy on anyone who turns from it (verses 14–17).

Obedience is next and has knocked at my door many, many times. I have been called to get out of my comfort zone more times than I feel is my share, and it comes in a couple of different ways: voluntary or involuntarily. Losing my anchoring job with CBS was involuntary. Signing off at my radio job of fourteen years was somewhere in between, and walking away from my radio syndication programming was with no doubt voluntary. Each time I was working and performing as contractually agreed, and each time I found that God was calling me away for His greater purpose. Obeying God is not by any means an easy road. As a matter of a fact, it is the toughest, roughest track on earth! There is no good time to lose or walk away from a job or commitment that you've put forth your best effort. However, the more God challenges you to surrender, trust, and obey, the clearer your path. I believe God tests our will to not only draw us near but to teach us how to be more like Him! It is His desire and promise to love, protect, and provide for us. He uses trials to expose the sin in our hearts, and when we turn to Him for redemption that is when we are able to fully receive the blessings He has in store for us. Let me say that again. When we turn to Christ for redemption, then we are able to fully receive the blessings God has planned for our lives!

The best tool for obedience is trusting Jesus—neither can succeed without the other. The Apostle John beautifully articulates, "But if anyone obeys his word, God's love is truly made complete in him. This is how we know we are in him: Whoever claims to live in him must walk as Jesus did" (1 John 2:5–6).

The fifth and final tool challenges your level of trust and is an essential part of your walk when it feels like life is crashing in around you. Hold on tight to patience and quiet time! Listen for the Lord to speak. Waiting around for answers is one of the most difficult aspects of the Christian life and requires tremendous faith.

I'm sure you would agree that it's hard to hear when there's a whole bunch of background noise. It's distracting and will blast God's clarity out the door every time. Rather than keeping ourselves so busy that we wouldn't be able to hear God if we wanted to, "Instead, it should be that of your inner self, the unfading beauty of a gentle and quiet spirit, which is of great worth in God's sight" (1 Peter 3:4). When we take time out for God, we will find Him there!

On the flipside, God is oftentimes patient with us! In 2 Peter 3:9, we learn, "The Lord is not slow in keeping his promise, as some understand slowness. He is patient with you, not wanting anyone to perish, but everyone to come to repentance."

The devil whispers the old cliché lie that there's *more than one way* to get to God. However, the truth is that we may all have a personal testimony, but there is only *one way* to God, and it's through the shed blood of His Son.

STUDY QUESTIONS

1. Do you believe Jesus is the Son of God?

2. What does God desire to have with *all* His creation?

3. Where is God when you're trying to avoid Him?

4. When have you claimed God's glory for your own?

5. What promise are we given in Romans 8:26–27?

6. Do you face any *impossibilities?*

Are you ready to put your complete faith in Christ? If so, please pray:

> Dear heavenly Father, I come to you as a sinner in need of a Savior. I confess my sin and ask that the shed blood of Jesus cleanse me of all wrongdoing and that I may live out the rest of my life according to Your perfect will, not my own. I believe Christ died so I may have eternal life by believing in His holy name. Please come into my heart, Lord Jesus. Amen!

7. Society pushes the mantra, "Trust no one but yourself." Do you agree or disagree?

8. List the two forms of obedience.

9. What tool will help you to choose obedience over sin?

10. How is trust challenged?

11. When has God patiently waited upon you?

12. When have you patiently waited upon God? What was the outcome?

13. There is one way to God but many ways to Christ. What is your testimony?

US

Thinking about us, you and me, indicates plural or more than one person. In God's eyes we were made to be together, not alone, and to live in community with one another. On the sixth day of Creation, "God created man in his own image, in the image of God he created him; male and female he created them" (Genesis 1:27). Now follow me on this one because I'm not a theologian, but the first chapter ends with God looking at all he had made that day "and it was very good" (verse 31). However, in Genesis 2:18, "The Lord God said, 'It is not good for the man to be alone. I will make a helper suitable for him.'" And Eve was created from a rib taken from Adam while he was in a deep sleep (verses 21–22).

Let's take a look at one particular root word in Hebrew that may help us figure this out together. First, God says everything that he made on the sixth day of Creation was very good, and a few verses later He retracted that a bit by saying the creation of Adam was not so good. So, which is it? According to my Archaeological Study Bible, the Hebrew word *toledôth* used in Genesis 2:4 means a subsequent or emergent account of something previously described or explained:

> This is the account (*toledôth*) of the heavens and the earth when they were created. When the Lord God made the earth and the heavens. (Italicized word is mine.)
>
> (Walter C. Kaiser and Garrett 2006)

While Genesis 1 gives us an *overview* of how the universe was created, Genesis 2:4–25 gives us further *insight* as to how man was created. It seems more like an aside that God uses to teach us how important it is to be in the presence of another. We can choose to be in His presence, as well as in the company of the flesh—friends and family—that He created for us to share in community. It is *not good* to be alone and *very good* to be together!

The *us,* for me, is often time spent with my dogs, not other people. In fact, I've done such a thorough job of protecting my personal business from others that I have gobs of business connections and little else. This is what I was talking about when I was sharing details of the kingdom of me. Before I knew it, I was alone and on my own, just as I had planned it!

Don't get me wrong; I love my dogs! At one time I had three cocker spaniels living under the same roof! "Woof, woof" was the operative phrase around here! They are my pride and joy, and I love spending my spare time caring for, walking, and bragging about them. Sage Advice was my first puppy out of college and the runt of his litter. I got him from a local breeder as a gift from my bunk bed buddy and brother-in-law for Christmas 1996. What a great day! At the breeder's house, this tiny yet mighty, black ball of fluff bounded past me and toward the Christmas tree. Thankfully, he didn't lift his leg! Then he came back to me and got his tiny paw caught in the carpet and yelped for help. I melted like a snowman; he was the perfect one for me!

I got Sage near the beginning of my radio career and spent long hours at work. He always met me at the door and was never out of my sight. When I first brought my sweet puppy home, he followed me everywhere, including the bathroom. When I'd step into the shower, I'd give him a puppy pep talk with my puppy voice and reassure him that he would be okay and that I would be out in a jiffy (dog speak)! One morning he got brave and snuggled his little, black nose through the curtain, slowly crept into the shower, plopped down in front of my feet and looked up into the showerhead at me with forlorn eyes. I couldn't help but laugh and scoop him into my arms. My sweet Sage didn't want to be alone, and at last he felt safe again! This went on for months until he caught on that this wasn't normal dog behavior, getting washed every day and all!

My idea of community centered on the people I worked with and my dog. If God wasn't getting the message to me through His Word, He was using Sage to tell me that even the creatures He created are not naturally wired to be alone. So I eventually adopted two abused or abandoned cocker spaniels through a couple of rescue programs. My female is black and white with polka dots down her back. I named her Spring Aire because I flew her home (Get it? Aire for flying through the air) the spring my nephew was born in Texas. I guess the reasoning was if my sister could have a baby, then so could I. Actually, the Dallas-Fort Worth Cocker Spaniel Rescue called my sister in hopes of finding a home because they were at capacity. Who could say no to a fluffy, polka-dotted puppy? Summer Adventure is a gorgeous, two-tone brown male and blind. My bunk bed buddy found him online, and, well, I went on an adventure to Wisconsin one summer day and brought him home, thus his namesake! Each time, I never gave it a thought that Sage would have a problem first with his new sister and later a brother. Sage seemed to really enjoy the company while I was away at work for hours on end.

Getting back to Genesis chapters one and two, God teaches us that it was *not good* to be alone and *very good* to have a partner. Clearly, I take that seriously when it comes to my dogs, but I'm still going it alone in my personal life. I've become so isolated from others that it took me getting on my knees before the Lord to confess my blatant disregard for the way He created me. I'm going against nature, and maybe you're agreeing with me and have found yourself in the same situation.

There's a really poignant proverb that many of our parents used when we were younger and not so popular in school. It's the lesson about having one friend who is far more valuable than many! Well, you can find their source in Proverbs 18:24: "A man of many companions may come to ruin, but there is a friend who sticks closer than a brother." Scripture teaches that some of us have tons of acquaintances but no intimacy, and those who have one friend have learned the key to defeating loneliness. Loneliness is everywhere, and the vicious cycle can be broken through community.

Further proof of how far our society will go to be alone is the latest data from the 2000 census. Did you know that the fastest-growing population of home ownership in America is single? For the first time in the history of information collected by the U.S. Census Bureau, single-family owners rank second to married couples followed by nonfamily households. More single women than men live alone with 56 percent of them owning their homes as compared to nearly half of the single men. Also, 6 percent of the entire population is *living together* with a nonrelative (Woodward and Damon 2001).

America is changing the way the world values community. More and more, we are avoiding commitment and remaining single to pursue other things, mainly self. The greater question becomes what do we do about avoiding isolation in the midst of the conveniences of communicating via Internet, cell phones, plus holding down a career, raising a family, our pets, and keeping up with the neighbors? At any given moment, there are a variety of things going on that truly distract us, and it's all leading to a breaking point. No one person can indefinitely handle the daily influx of information that is bombarding our e-mail, cell phones, television screens, airwaves, work, school, and home life.

Intimate interaction is becoming extinct, and it's gotten to the point that employers are firing loyal employees by e-mail or texting. Married couples are arguing online to avoid face-to-face confrontation. Personal occasional cards or announcements are being replaced by e-cards and e-vites, and although some form of this way of communication helps us keep within a certain budget and saves a few trees, physical and verbal skills are seriously lacking, and our relationships are starting to suffer because of it. We need more *us*, and getting into the Word can lead us to answers on how to do it!

Immersing yourself in the Gospels of Matthew, Mark, Luke, and John is a good place to start your biblical journey. They are found in the first four books of the New Testament. Matthew and John were both disciples of Jesus while John and Mark traveled with the Apostle Paul and Barnabas during his first missionary trip. Luke was a doctor and the only known Gentile author in the New Testament. In addition to the book of Luke, which highlights the compassion Jesus showed people, particularly women, he also penned the book of Acts. Luke was a friend of Paul's and traveled with him on mission trips as well. Paul is an appointed apostle and key teacher of Christ, and we see him following Jesus' example by being in community and traveling with at least one other person on all of his journeys. Some of the attributes of community include a second perspective or viewpoint, accountability, witness, shared experiences, and camaraderie, much like the inspired gospels of Jesus' life with the disciples.

Have you noticed a pattern about being in true relationship with God, Jesus, and the Holy Spirit? We are never alone or apart from Him. Jesus taught in John 15:1, "I am the true vine, and my Father is the gardener." Later, He said, "I am the vine; you are the branches. If a man remains in me and I in him, he will bear much fruit; apart from me you can do nothing" (verse 5). We can stray and pursue ambition on our own (Galatians 5:17) or we can return to Jesus and bear fruit like peace, joy, love, patience, kindness, goodness, faithfulness, gentleness, and self-control (Galatians 5:22–23). The fruit of the Spirit speaks to me in that these are the qualities of the kind of person I want to be. The Bible is right: "The acts of the sinful nature are obvious" (Galatians 5:19), like jealousy, fits of rage, and selfish ambition and are quite honestly the easy road for all of us to take. There's no commitment required, no community for support, and no one to hold us accountable for our actions.

Jesus promises us in Matthew 18:19–20, "Again, I

tell you that if two of you on earth agree about anything you ask for, it will be done for you by my Father
in heaven. For where two or three come together in my
name, there am I with them."

Yes! This is how God speaks and comes to life in
us. I love these verses too. Jesus promises to be the One
who goes to the Father with our prayer requests when
we call on His name together. Remember when God
said it is *not good* to be alone in Genesis 2? God and
Jesus are on the same page here! Now it's our turn to
get on board because the more we do things His way
(obedience) the deeper our relationship goes with Him
and others. Note that I included *us* in that last sentence. When we draw closer to God by following His
command to worship in community, we are serving
Him, building the body, and gaining support in our
lives. Three things come from one effort.

I think getting together with one or two other people has additional benefits. For example, Jesus mentions we will get what we ask for "if two of you on earth
agree about anything" (verse 19). *If* indicates a conditional outcome. It is up to us to work out our differing
agendas before going to Jesus with our heart's desire.
Second, agreeing on something with another believer
may involve praying separately for God's will to be
done before coming together and submitting a request.
In any event, it is a process of considering each person's
needs, thoughts, and feelings by keeping one another
accountable according to Scripture. When we're on the
same page, God has our full attention. More impor-
tantly, when God answers our agreed upon prayer, we

know that it could only have come from Him and all praise points back to Him!

Each time I visit my bunk bed buddy, we get together with an amazing woman who can only be described as a prayer warrior. Her heart is on fire for God, and when she calls on Jesus to stand in our presence, you can feel His power. It's awesome! So awesome, in fact, that I decided I had never quite invited Jesus into my prayer life like that before and did two things: I joined a prayer group at my church to learn how to serve Him through the body, and I now verbally call on His name during my personal time of worship. There's something about shouting "Jesus!" out loud, and it truly brings glory to His name. God deserves our praise, and He asks us to do it often. Here are few community praises from the Old and New Testaments:

> Praise the Lord. How good it is to sing praises to our God, how pleasant and fitting to praise him!
>
> Psalm 147:1

> Praise be to the Lord, the God of Israel, from everlasting to everlasting. Then all the people said "Amen" and "Praise the Lord."
>
> 1 Chronicles 16:36

> The trumpeters and singers joined in unison, as with one voice, to give praise and thanks to the Lord. Accompanied by trumpets, cymbals and other instruments, they raised their voices in praise to the Lord and sang: "He is good; his love endures forever." Then the temple of the Lord

was filled with a cloud, and the priests could not perform their service because of the cloud, for the glory of the Lord filled the temple of God.

2 Chronicles 5:13–14

As they began to sing and praise, the Lord set ambushes against the men of Ammon and Moab and Mount Seir who were invading Judah, and they were defeated.

2 Chronicles 20:22

In a loud voice they sang: "Worthy is the Lamb, who was slain, to receive power and wealth and wisdom and strength and honor and glory and praise!"

Revelation 5:12

Things begin to happen when two or more people come together to praise the Lord! He hears us calling and shows up! I don't know about you, but I'd like to have that kind of relationship with God, and the first step is learning how to deny *me* in exchange for more *we*.

ME AND HIM

Everyone is a survivor. Some of us are better at keeping our heads above water than others, but given flood conditions, we all have that instinct to fight for air and weather the storm. I recently dug up my old diaries that date back to my college and early professional years. Some of the events I described seem like they happened yesterday and others I've completely forgotten about. Like this entry:

> My faith needs to be stronger. God, why am I holding myself back from you? Why am I in my own little world—lonely, scared—yet I realize how fortunate I am and feel I should be rejoicing? I guess I'm human, and nothing ever seems to be quite right… hmmm… Lord, lead me, walk with me, love me.
>
> November 19, 1992

First jobs are tough, and this was written just six months after college graduation. A lot was going on, and I was trying to be everything to everyone, including God. Looking back on this makes me so sad because I can see the holes in everything I put on paper. Sure, I was frustrated and burning out, but I was also trying to force my relationship with God by excusing my lack of faith and asking Him to take care of me. The survivor in me failed to fully surrender and praise Him, putting me first, not Him.

If you're new in your walk with Christ, like I once was, you may be experiencing some of the same feelings. Let me guess: when you pray, you don't understand why God isn't snapping His fingers to get you what you want when you want it, right? I admit that it would be great to see such quick results, but the results would be temporary, and God asks us to come to Him in a totally different way. By accepting Christ as Savior, we not only confess our sins, ask for forgiveness, and work to turn from sin (repentance), we also acknowledge that *God is in control of all things.* We humbly come to Him in prayer and petition, asking Him what He has in store rather than what we want. God isn't a lottery ticket; He is our Creator, and He knows our every need.

I feel like it's time to have another heart-to-heart discussion about how to have a personal relationship with Christ. You are not in trouble for asking God to meet your needs. In fact, God asks us to come to Him for all things. We get into trouble when we deny what Christ did at the cross by continually choosing to turn inward for guidance. That's what I was doing when I wrote in my journal that I was *holding back.* The good news is that I was somewhat aware of my attitude toward my relationship with Him and was crying for help. The bad news is that I had initially put Christ second to the throne of me and was reaping a whole lot of discord and unhappiness before I went to Him for guidance.

When spiritual stumbling occurs, our first response should always be to surrender to God. If you're not there yet, try paying attention to the things that trigger you to control a situation before you think to go to God with it. Some of my triggers include not having a good grasp of the Scripture, being caught off guard, or plain, old selfishness. To surrender, pray God's will, not your own, especially when you're confused about something.

I don't ever want to fall into Satan's trap of handling

something before I go to God with it. Traps are oftentimes subtle, but you can be sure that they are from Satan and *not* God, including doubt, fear, temptation, confusion, and distraction. It's too dangerous to rely on myself to make the right choice without praying about it first. I've learned one too many tough lessons doing anything differently. We all have weak moments, and those are the times the devil and his crazy demons attack, so pray that the Holy Spirit always brings you to the truth of a matter. He is the best guide!

The more I study the Bible, the more I'm in awe of what God has done to show me His love. Jesus is our teacher, who, in Luke 10:21, shows us how to properly go to God: "At that time Jesus, full of joy through the Holy Spirit, said, 'I praise you, Father, Lord of heaven and earth.'" Filled with the fruit of the Spirit, joy, Jesus first praises God and then acknowledges His sovereignty! Now that's reverence, and Jesus is showing us how to humbly go to the Father in praise. There is no *me* in praising God. We need to sacrifice self to Christ, giving Him the throne He so deserves.

HIM AND ME

Surrender is a controversial word. In times of war, it is a dishonorable act of defeat, but in a relationship with Christ, it is essential to spiritual growth. Oddly enough, if you choose to delve deep into a relationship with Christ, surrender will be your daily battle against the desires of the flesh. To be sure, surrendering your agenda to God has the potential to physically, emotionally, and spiritually wear you out if you don't stop and learn how to do it as Jesus taught us. Surrendering requires getting into the Word, prayer, and laying your life out before the Lord.

Nothing is off limits to God when we truly surrender. I think that statement requires a yikes and a half! Did I just say that surrender means allowing God to take complete control of my life? Answer: yes, I did! Okay, take a moment and collect your thoughts and commit to prayer your desire to surrender control of your life over to God one day at a time. Since this may be new territory for you, start with baby steps by *writing out a covenant* between you and God. It may say something like, "Lord, I want to surrender all areas of my life over to you. I can't do that on my own and promise to come to you in prayer each time I feel like I'm trying to take control of my circumstances. I ask that you substitute my tendency to control with Your peace. Amen." Whatever your covenant says, pray over it and submit it to Him in prayer as often as it takes to know His peace. Pretty soon, you will have a light-bulb moment and be one baby step closer to full surrender!

So far, we've learned that God wants us to be in community by surrounding ourselves with other believers who are building up the body of Christ. Not only are we being lifted up by their spiritual gifts, but we're also using ours to bear fruit (refer back to chapter "3D"). A few fruits of the Spirit include joy, love, kindness, and self-control. When we accept Christ as Savior, we are admitting our sinful nature and by doing so relinquish the throne of *self* to Christ. Now and forever, He belongs at the center of our lives; otherwise, we are not truly transformed. Our light will go dim like what briefly happened to Paul's protégé, Timothy, and our walk with Christ will come to a complete standstill. The acts of the sinful nature like selfish ambition and fits of rage will sneak into our lives and take over like an overgrown briar patch!

Times were pretty intense while the first churches were being planted after Christ's death and resurrection. Believers like Stephen were being martyred for their faith. Hatred for believers was at an historical high; all the while, Paul was preaching the gospel and teaching followers like Timothy to stand firm and do the same. In 2 Timothy 2:22–26, Paul writes from prison:

> Flee the evil desires of youth, and pursue righteousness, faith, love and peace, along with those who call on the Lord (surrender) out of a pure heart. Don't have anything to do with foolish and stupid arguments, because you know they produce quarrels. And the Lord's servant must not quarrel; instead, he must be kind to everyone, able to teach, not resentful. Those who oppose him he must gently instruct, in the hope that God will grant them repentance leading them to a knowledge of the truth, and that they will come to their senses and escape from the trap of the devil, who has taken them captive to do his will. (Surrender is my own word)

Timothy needed encouragement, and Paul laid these nuggets o' wisdom at his doorstep! First, he advised him to surrender his evil desires to Christ and fill his heart with all of the good stuff. He pointed out that arguments are bad, but showing kindness during a disagreement is the equivalent of heaping hot coals on the head of the enemy, which protects the heart from doing evil in return. Finally, and this is his advice for how to relate to all who are lost, Paul tells us to gently instruct or witness and then surrender that person over to God. We cannot change what people believe; however, we can ask God to lead them to a knowledge of the truth (Colossians 1:9).

Personal surrender is a full-time job, and Paul confirms that we're only responsible for our own actions. Address personal goals to surrender, and you will begin choosing kindness over anger and Christ over self.

You will soon notice that the tools of life are pretty much always the same and that surrender is the first key. Of course, our experience with everyday issues and circumstances are continually in a state of flux, but how we approach or handle them should remain constant. Think of it this way: if God is unchanging and we have Christ filling us with His Spirit to guide us, then we should be able to stand firm as well! Commit this verse to memory as a daily reminder of God's unwavering power and love: "He is the Rock, his works are perfect, and all his ways are just. A faithful God who does no wrong, upright and just is he" (Deuteronomy 32:4).

STUDY QUESTIONS

1. In Hebrew, *toledôth* means a subsequent or emergent account of something previously described or explained. How do Genesis chapters one and two complement the other?

2. On a scale of one to ten, are you more isolated, balanced, or social?

3. How do you fill the void in your life (who or what)?

4. If you were to peel away all the layers of business associates, neighbors, and acquaintances, whom would you find in your community?

5. Would you agree or disagree that you value being by yourself more than committing to others? Why?

6. Find Scripture that instructs *us* how to relate to one another in community. (For example, 1 Corinthians 12:12–31)

7. Describe how you know you are in a true relationship with God, Christ, and the Holy Spirit.

8. Comparing the fruits of the Spirit and the acts of the sin nature outlined in Galatians 5, what sin do you need to switch out to only bear fruit?

9. How do we know God hears our prayers? Read Matthew 18:19–20.

10. List one benefit of being in community with other believers.

11. When has God shown up during your prayers?

12. Have you ever tried to force God to *work for you* by demanding certain results?

13. List any frustration with your prayer life.

14. Discuss ways you can change how you pray and listen for God to answer by sharing at least one solution.

15. Who should believers initially go to for guidance and how can you keep self in check?

16. Identify a few triggers that lead to taking personal control of a situation.

17. How can you change your behavior or tendency to control?

18. What are the subtle traps you frequently face?

19. What steps do you need to take to learn surrender?

20. Is it possible to change what other people believe?

21. Who are we responsible for?

22. What helps us stand firm?

PART THREE

HOW ABOUT YOU?
WHAT DO YOU BELIEVE?

Are you sitting down right now? If yes, please stand up and walk to the nearest mirror. I'll wait! Okay, spend a couple of minutes looking over your entire body and describe what you see. A person who is more approachable or hard? Do you see a particular relative more and more each day, and if so, is this a good thing? Maybe you look better than you have in a while or maybe you've never looked more tired.

What you see in the mirror may be a result of the condition of your heart. Ask yourself what you believe in your understanding and relationship with Christ. It's time to uproot worldly relative truth and replace it with the absolute truth of God's Word. It's also time to stop treating the Bible as a smorgasbord by choosing what commands and promises you feel like following and then ignoring the rest.

How many of us have said, "I believe this, but I don't

understand or want any part of that?" The moment we attempt to break down Scripture to fit our understanding we are on the path to religion, not faith in Christ. God knows us so well and is all about forgiveness when we stumble. After delivering His people out of slavery in Egypt and forty years of wandering the desert because of rebellion, God warned the Israelites through Moses, "See that you do all I command you; do not add to it or take away from it" (Deuteronomy 12:32). The lesson we all need to learn before God brings us to the promised land is to choose to fully obey His commands, put our trust in Jesus, and wait for deliverance. Picking and choosing what we will or will not believe is not total surrender and submission to Christ; it's the religion of self.

As followers of Christ, we have a covenant with God to pursue His plan for our lives, not our own. By doing so, we understand that in good times and bad He has a purpose and plan for our lives that far exceeds anything we could ever do in our own strength. Are you being managed by your own ideals, or does Jesus have the reigns of your heart?

I can tell you that He didn't have complete hold of me until He pulled me in not too long ago. I may have even heard a slight "Whoa, Bessie!" before I was aware of His calling. Earlier, I shared with you that I had started my own company with five partners prior to losing my morning radio job but again found myself at a crossroads. Eleven months into it, I had already flown with one other partner to Dallas and New York and driven to Minneapolis and Detroit to present my idea, and all of a sudden it came to a grinding halt. Looking back, it's because God was testing whether or not I would trust taking a new direction that He had been planning for me, a plan that would take me away from a project I had spent nearly a year putting my blood, sweat, and tears into with no salary and no satisfaction of the fruits of my labor. Talk about who's in control! God had me chomping at the bit!

It was a relief when He spoke to me again on November 14, 2008, and said, "Sabrina, nothing depends on other people; it all depends on Me." I so needed to hear that! I needed for God to lift the tremendous burden of the success of my new job running a business off of my shoulders. I also learned that nothing depends on Sabrina. My plate was full, and I was feeling the pressure to deliver results and fast! Without even trying, I was slowly putting God back on that shelf and taking over His rightful throne in my life.

God used the one partner who had challenged what God had to do with running a business to get my focus back on Him. It weighed on my heart as I prayed for clarity for the next right step. For six weeks, crickets could be heard throughout my house while I was on my knees before the Lord. It was my time to be still and patiently wait. Meanwhile, I had confided in my bunk bed buddy and one other person, who each led me to separate scripture (2 Chronicles 20:35–37 and 2 Corinthians 6:14) that warned against entering into a partnership with this man. Thanksgiving weekend, I officially walked away from the business out of obedience to Christ.

At an earlier point in my life, I wouldn't have been faithfully trusting in God enough to skip the question "Why" or "Why me?" In fact, I would have kept running the business and undoubtedly right into the ground. Guess who would have reveled in my demise? Instead there was only one choice: to obey God's will. I knew in my heart what He was asking me to do, and I answered His call with humility and praise.

People who practice religion are best described as *doers*. "If I do this, I should be good with [insert god/idol of choice]" or, "I feel good about myself when I [insert action]." The more deeds you can take credit for, like bringing a needy family a bag of groceries or taking an elderly person to a doctor's appointment, the more you can add to your good name. The difference between followers of Christ and religious people is that God receives all the glory, not the individual. Jesus actually defines what we need to *do* when He answered His disciples in John 6:28–29: "Then they asked him, 'What must we do to do the works God requires?'

Jesus answered, 'The work of God is this: to believe in the one he has sent.'"

Scripture also commands us, "As the body without the spirit is dead, so faith without deeds is dead" (James 2:26). Deeds of faith are the fruits and gifts of our commitment to do for Christ as He has done for us. Further, Ephesians 2:10 tells us where deeds come from: "For we are God's workmanship, created in

Christ Jesus to do good works, which God prepared in advance for us to do."

We've already been assigned how to best serve with the gifts we've been given and enter the danger zone when we compartmentalize, change, or dismiss God's Word to fit our lifestyle. Paul best describes such people as "having a form of godliness but denying its power" (2 Timothy 3:5). Who's the manager of your life? You? Someone else? Jesus?

YOU ARE WHO?

I desperately want to visit the Whoville that Dr. Seuss describes in *How the Grinch Stole Christmas!* What a place. Everyone is happy, even when they wake up to zero Christmas presents and the Who Hash is gone! As a kid, I was sure that this was what true Christmas spirit was all about and always looked forward to hearing Cindy Lou Who's soft voice as she joined hands with the others to sing, sing, sing!

The nonfictional Grinch (Satan) is forever on the prowl and always has a plan of attack. If he can rob you of the joy in your heart, he will do it! That's why it's important to learn who you are in Christ, how you're wired to serve His kingdom, and avoid being struck down by the enemy. A few of his strategies include fear or placing doubt in your mind of whether or not God can really be trusted with every drop of control in your life.

Walk with me back to the mirror and take a good, second look at yourself. Are you smiling or are you expressionless? How are your eyes? Are they twinkling or are they hollow? Since our insides aren't visible in a mirror image, how are you feeling while you're assessing your overall appearance? Satisfied, angry, embarrassed, sad, concerned, or maybe not quite sure? What is crossing your mind as you're making a mental note of your body?

At first glance in my mirror, I see a sincere woman with a few signs of aging, rosy cheeks, and a slight smile. My glass is always full (of coffee)! What's going through my mind is a whole other story with three or four ongoing themes, including prayer, lists of things to do today, and for the rest of the week. I'm constantly thinking about completing something or reaching a goal I've set for myself; all the while I'm assessing how I look from three different angles! If you have kids, a job, family members, or friends that are in your life, I'm sure they're also jogging through your mind 24/7 as well! We have a lot to think about, and it all starts to add up, doesn't it?

Since narcissism is an unattractive quality, let's all step away from the mirror for now and reach for our spiritual toolbox. There are three things we need to do to protect our heart, and we're going to need five tools to do it! You already know about faith and surrender. The other three include: obedience, trust, and patience.

First, you need to go to God and ask for forgiveness for any outstanding personal sin. Before you do that, make sure you have the tool of faith in your right hand and the tools of surrender and obedience in the left.

Second, you need to ask God to reveal any unresolved issues you may have with other people in your life. For this step, you'll definitely need obedience, trust, surrender, faith, and keep the patience tool on hand. This process could take time because it involves asking another person(s) for forgiveness and requires reconciliation. Third, you'll need the tools of faith, obedience, and trust to get more involved, to serve others, and to surround yourself with godly people in community as God commands.

Now before you either say, "No way. I can't possibly do all these things!" or "I don't have any of those issues." Remember that it is your choice to either walk away and continue depending on yourself or to step up to the plate and start putting Christ at the center of your life. It's that simple-hard: simple to let go, hard to continue surrendering self to Christ.

Asking God for forgiveness of sin that you've since swept under the carpet is a bold step in your new walk! The word *vulnerable* comes to mind. However, by laying your life before the Lord to weed any outstanding sin, you have already glorified God by surrendering your way to His. He loves it when we come to Him with a sincere heart because He hates the sin that separates us from having a true relationship. However, if we choose not to confess our sin, He cannot force us. We have the free will to harbor sin until the day we die, and Satan is counting on it!

Dependence is a better word for vulnerable because

the latter means that you're susceptible to attack, and when we surrender to Christ, He promises that we can depend on Him for all things, including protection! Letting go of the ugly sin in your life leads to a whole relationship with God. It's not an unstable, broken one.

For years I told myself that I didn't have any past regrets until one day while I was praying before bedtime and the tears started rolling down my face. All of a sudden it occurred to me that I was telling myself a complete lie just so I could continue living within my comfort zone. I had always reasoned that I never purposely hurt anyone, lied, or cheated in any way. But the truth is there have been times when I haven't told the whole story or ignored a conflict with someone until enough time had passed and bygones had become bygones. The moment I realized I was living in sin, I was ashamed and was on my knees before the Lord asking for forgiveness and help in reconciling my sin. We must deal with all sin because to ignore it is to give Satan a stronghold in our lives. Further confirmation of the need to root out all sin is found in 1 John 1:8 through 2:3:

> If we claim to be without sin, we deceive ourselves and the truth is not in us. If we confess our sins, he is faithful and just and will forgive us our sins and purify us from all unrighteousness. If we claim we have not sinned, we make him out to be a liar and his word has no place in our lives. My dear children, I write this to you so that you will not sin. But if anybody does sin, we have one who

speaks to the Father in our defense—Jesus Christ, the Righteous One. He is the atoning sacrifice for our sins, and not only for ours but also for the sins of the whole world.

If you're scared at the thought of putting your heart under God's microscope, don't be! Any emptiness or fear is not of God but Satan himself. He does not want you to deal with your sin because that would mean he loses his power over your life. Satan is the only one who seeks to destroy. Christ wants to restore you to Himself and guide you to the truth in the Holy Spirit. The Holy Spirit works through our conscience and supernaturally gives us what we lack, like grace, mercy, strength, or courage. Here are a couple of His promises:

> Now it is God who has made us for this very purpose and has given us the Spirit as a deposit, guaranteeing what is to come.
>
> 2 Corinthians 5:5

> Those who live according to the sinful nature have their minds set on what that nature desires; but those who live in accordance with the Spirit have their minds set on what the Spirit desires. The mind of sinful man is death, but the mind controlled by the Spirit is life and peace.
>
> Romans 8:5–6

CONFESSING SIN

While the tools of faith, surrender, and obedience are essential in rooting out sin, you may also want to equip yourself with trust and patience, as the Lord reveals both individual and unresolved sin involving other people. To get started, find a quiet place where you can get on your knees and pray. Kneeling before God shows reverence and puts Him at the center of your confession. Dealing with sin is not a fun process and can be quite intimidating; however, the Holy Spirit will guide you through the cleansing steps of confession, forgiveness, and redemption.

While I'm kneeling, I pray that God reveal any sin that I may have pushed to the back of my mind. Then I ask that He forgive me for not dealing with it and ask that He help me to avoid making the same mistake in the future. James 5:15–16 says, "And the prayer offered in faith will make the sick person well; the Lord will raise him up. If he has sinned, he will be forgiven. Therefore confess your sins to each other and pray for each other so that you may be healed. The prayer of the righteous man is powerful and effective." Facing personal sin glorifies God, and the Lord promises to forgive us when we confess and turn from it.

A second area of sin is the kind that involves a conflict with someone else. Dealing with personal sin is a piece of cake compared to reconciling with others! If God puts a conflict involving someone else on your heart, then you will need to take action by following the principles laid out in Matthew 7:3–5 and Matthew 18:15–18:

Why do you look at the speck of sawdust in your brother's eye and pay no attention to the plank in your own eye? How can you say to your brother, 'Let me take the speck out of your eye,' when all the time there is a plank in your own eye? You hypocrite, first take the plank out of your own eye, and then you will see clearly to remove the speck from your brother's eye…If your brother sins against you, go and show him his fault, just between the two of you. If he listens to you, you have won your brother over. But if he will not listen, take one or two others along, so that 'every matter may be established by the testimony of two or three witnesses.' If he refuses to listen to them, tell it to the church; and if he refuses to listen even to the church, treat him as you would a pagan or a tax collector. "I tell you the truth, whatever you bind on earth will be bound in heaven, and whatever you loose on earth will be loosed in heaven."

As awkward as it may seem to go to another person, remember that these are the very words Jesus spoke to His disciples about how to handle conflict His way. I've had some pretty amazing experiences with following both passages and have found that God not only reconciles me to the person but also gives me an indescribable peace afterward. Warning: the person you are in conflict with may not feel the same. Reconciliation isn't a feeling; it is an act of obedience. If he or she is not humbled by the same act of obedience, then you may experience a pull on his or her part to place blame back onto you or to win the fight. If he or she walks away from you, continue to pray for reconciliation and ask God to restore your relationship. Despite the outcome of the reconciliation process, you will still have peace for honoring God.

Identifying your part in a conflict is essential to the reconciliation process. Make sure you allow God to show you where you need to confess sin before you go to the other person. If your expectation is to walk away from a conflict without taking personal responsibility for your actions, then you will not have true reconciliation. Christ has to be at the center of all conflict resolution, not you.

Physically going to another person is key in getting through the conflict as God intended. E-mailing, texting, talking on your cell or landline is not a great idea unless you're trying to set a date and place to meet for your discussion. When I was led to confront my former business partner about a disconcerting statement he had made, I e-mailed my request for a face-to-face meeting. He agreed and we talked at a coffee shop. I did so for two reasons: out of respect for my partner and to give the importance due my concern. Following Scripture allows the Holy Spirit to guide you to the truth of a conflict and is much more than going through the motions. Working through your sin is a cleansing process (sanctification). If we deny God the glory of reconciliation, we remain in our sin and dig ourselves into a pit residing with Satan.

Until you choose to stomp out sin God's way, you will sacrifice peace for unrest and unconditional loving relationships for dysfunctional ones at best. Getting on your knees before the Lord is so awesome, and He will never abandon you for putting Him at the center of your desire to confess personal sin and hurt.

SERVING GOD

A final and ongoing strand of your relationship with Christ involves rolling up your sleeves to serve. I'm a newcomer to serving with others and prefer one-on-one opportunities. You may be completely opposite and already have your hand in a variety of activities, and that's great, as long as your focus is serving the body, not being seen doing it! We must abide in Christ, which means He is allowed to work in and through us (John 15:1–8). If we're simply involved and there's no divine connection, then we're only serving ourselves. A good rule of thumb is to pray for God to show you where He can best use your spiritual gift(s) to serve the church community. If you aren't sure what your gifts are, I encourage you to access the link located at the back of this book and take the online test (Gilbert 2009). Your church may also have a spiritual gifts assessment program that may be even more helpful in getting you where you need to be.

Pray for godly friends as well. As essential to the body as it is to serve, God also created us to be in the very good company of others (Genesis 1:31)!

"For where two or three are gathered together in my name, there am I with them" (Matthew 18:20).

If the idea of pursuing these three areas of your life has convicted you today, praise God! You are on the path of peace and purpose through the saving grace of Jesus.

This is from the heart of a little boy from Mexico who learned about Christ through the Samaritan's Purse Operation Christmas Child program:

> I was a troublemaker; that is what people said. When I started to study the Bible lessons and put my trust in Jesus, my life changed. Now I know that somebody cares for me, I want to be a good boy. I am going to do anything that Jesus asks me to do.
>
> (Graham 2009)

Only Peter can add to this sweet child's message by saying, "As obedient children, do not be conformed to the former lusts which were yours in your ignorance, but like the Holy One who called you, be holy yourselves also in all your behavior" (1 Peter 1:14–15).

STUDY QUESTIONS

1. How have you tried to manage your relationship with Christ?

2. Are you religious or a person of faith? Explain.

3. Is your relationship with Christ more centered on His teachings or your personal experiences?

4. Share a recent "Whoa, Bessie" moment!

5. Obedience comes with a price. Do you believe it leads to your demise or reward?

6. Are you a *doer* or a *glorifier?*

7. Who do you answer to in life? (You, someone else, Christ?)

8. Currently, can you say you know true joy or are you usually discontent?

9. What will God reveal to you when you ask forgiveness?

10. Identify a holding pattern or comfort zone.

11. What is the difference between Christ and Satan?

12. What benefit could possibly come from facing personal sin?

13. Are you in conflict with someone else? Explain who.

14. What comes of biblical reconciliation?

15. What responsibility in your current conflict is your own?

16. What processes do we go through by dealing with sin and who is glorified?

17. How can you abide in Christ?

18. What three areas of life are covered in this chapter?

YOU, YOURSELF, AND HIM

A few years after my nephew, Storm, was born in Texas, my sister (bunk bed buddy) and brother-in-law moved to Minnesota. Talk about climate change! I remember discussing how the sun doesn't shine every day in the north like it does in the South, to which my sister said, "I can't wait!"

"What?" I asked. "You're looking forward to gloomy days and long winters?"

"Yep," she said. "I'm really looking forward to enjoying all four seasons, and I don't mind the clouds and snow that come with it!" Soon after settling in, I went for a visit, and my nephew insisted we go on a nature walk and admire all of the beautiful surrounding lakes and trails.

I giggle every time I think of our first fall adventure into the woods. What a hoot! Storm tucked his pants into his designer froggie rain boots, grabbed a pail, and sand shovel, and off we went on our nature walk! We collected everything from leaves to grasshoppers; all the while he was humming a sweet song he had learned in preschool. Precious. Then I got to thinking about nature, as in a person's individual nature, and was led to scripture in Romans 8:1–2 about life through the Spirit: "Therefore, there is now no condemnation for those who are in Christ Jesus, because through Christ Jesus the law of the Spirit of life set me free from the law of sin and death."

Jesus is our all-encompassing freedom. We are not doomed. The only death sentence we face is to our body, like everyone else. Try comprehending what is promised here. Life begins the moment we accept Christ as Savior and continues even after our physical death. Hope conquers hopelessness! When we are in Christ, His Spirit begins to lead us on our nature walk and changes our course from raging, slandering, using filthy language, and telling lies to clothing us with compassion, kindness, humility, gentleness, and patience (Colossians 3:8–12).

Writing this book has been an incredible blessing in that I have had the unique opportunity to share Christ with a variety of people I wouldn't normally reach during my day-to-day activities. Usually, I would wait to share my love for Him after getting to know someone a bit better and surely it would have to happen over a cup of coffee! However, each time I say that I've written a book and have been blessed with a publisher, there is immediate curiosity about its premise, and it opens the door to sharing the plan of salvation! Isn't this how God really works?

One recurring response to me describing *Faith and the S.T.O.P. Principle* comes in the form of the question, "Do you really believe Jesus is equal to God?" A photographer friend of mine actually asked that question, and I answered, "Yes, Jesus is God in the flesh and was sent by God the Father to reveal His character and love for His creation. The purpose for Jesus' life on earth was to fulfill Old Testament prophecy of a Messiah who would conquer sin and death with His own life. Christ is the unblemished Lamb of Life and Savior of all who choose to call on His name. He is the only One who has paid our sin debt in full by His shed blood on the cross at Calvary."

Just before Jesus was arrested and nailed to the cross with all of our sin, He answered my photographer friend in John 14:6: "I am the way and the truth and the life. No one comes to the Father except through me." After His resurrection, Peter took what Jesus said in John 14:6 and went before the Sanhedrin (the same Jewish council that sentenced Jesus to death) in Jerusalem. In Acts 4:8–12, we learn:

> Then Peter, filled with the Holy Spirit, said to them: "Rulers and elders of the people! If we are being called to account today for an act of kindness shown to a cripple and are asked how he was healed, then know this, you and all the people of Israel: It is by the name of Jesus Christ of Nazareth, whom you crucified but whom God raised from the dead, that this man stands before you healed.

He is 'the stone you builders rejected, which has become the capstone.' Salvation is found in no one else, for there is no other name under heaven given to men by which we must be saved."

Peter quotes Psalm 118:22 to reveal that Jesus is the capstone! Notice that scripture tells us that he was filled with the Holy Spirit. The Holy Spirit is otherwise known as the Counselor and a deposit of the Spirit of Christ in all who profess faith in Him. The Holy Spirit is also equal to God, and we learn more about the gift of the Spirit just before Jesus ascends into heaven. While Jesus is preparing His disciples for His crucifixion, He promised, "But the Counselor, the Holy Spirit, whom the Father will send in my name, will teach you all things and will remind you of everything I have said to you. And with that he breathed on them and said, "Receive the Holy Spirit"" (John 14:26, 20:22).

If you're scratching your head and still have questions about the authority of God, Christ, and the Holy Spirit, go with me back to Genesis 2:7. It says, "The Lord God formed the man from the dust of the ground and breathed into his nostrils the breath of life, and the man became a living being." After reading this passage, what gives us life? If you answered God's breath or Spirit, then you were right! Now let's reexamine John 20:22. What happened when Jesus breathed on the disciples? You answered correctly if you said Jesus' Spirit came upon them! Both God and Christ give life through their Spirit. God breathed life into man, and

Jesus breathes eternal life into all believers with His Holy Spirit.

Follow me to scripture in Acts 2:36–38 for further understanding. Once again, Peter is spreading the gospel of Christ and says:

> "Therefore let all Israel be assured of this: God has made this Jesus, whom you crucified, both Lord and Christ." When the people heard this, they were cut to the heart and said to Peter and the other apostles, "Brothers, what shall we do?" Peter replied, "Repent and be baptized, every one of you, in the name of Jesus Christ for the forgiveness of your sins. And you will receive the gift of the Holy Spirit."

But wait! The clincher comes next when Peter says in verse 39, "The promise is for you and your children and for all who are far off—for all whom the Lord our God will call." He's talking about you and me here! Jew or Gentile, we are all promised the gift of the Holy Spirit through faith in Christ. Peter also assures us that God made Jesus both Lord and Christ, equating Jesus to the Lord our God. Pretty exciting, isn't it?

My photographer friend parted that day with this statement: "I think knowing that Christ is God is what a lot of Christians don't understand." She's so right, and the absolute true answer is in God's Word. God said that Jesus is His Son (Mark 9:7) and Jesus said, "I tell you the truth, whoever hears my word and believes him who sent me has eternal life and will not be condemned; he has crossed over from death to life" (John

5:24). Then we have a choice to make. It is the only question with eternal value attached to the answer! Are you going to continue living for self or turn from your sin to live for the Savior? Regardless of which part of the world you live in, we are all on a nature walk with either our sin (you and yourself) or in the Spirit (you and Him).

SIN VERSUS SPIRIT

The power of our sin nature is pretty daunting at times but truly leads us on a death march if we continue living for this world. Paul wrote the book of Romans while he was traveling west during his third missionary trip and probably in Corinth. Prior to the scripture quoted in Romans 8 is his explanation of our inherent struggle with sin:

> I know that nothing good lives in me, that is, in my sinful nature. For I have the desire to do what is good, but I cannot carry it out. For what I do is not the good I want to do; no, the evil I do not want to do—this I keep on doing. Now if I do what I do not want to do, it is no longer I who do it, but it is sin living in me that does it.
>
> Romans 7:18–20

Paul concludes that although our sin nature will always battle God's law, we are set free through the law of the Spirit of life in Christ Jesus (Romans 8:2). Once again, we are faced with a choice to surrender our sin nature or to wallow in it and go it alone.

Many of us have heard of actor/producer/director Mel Gibson, who has a résumé that ranges from his wild days of the *Mad Max* or *Lethal Weapon* series to his behind-the-scenes work with *The Passion of the Christ*. Shortly thereafter, he publicly apologized for driving drunk and making an anti-Semitic comment to an officer of the law. Good or bad behavior aside, Gibson admitted, "I had always believed in God, that He existed. But in my middle years, I kind of drifted, and other things took center stage. At that point, I realized I needed something more if I was going to survive" (Comfort 2004).

Gibson, like many of us, has at one time or another put God on a shelf. It wasn't until he learned a couple of hard life lessons that he was willing to examine what was on center stage: self, not Christ. I do not know Gibson's heart anymore than I know yours, but God does, and He can't work with fractions. You are either all in (with the Spirit as your guide) or you are all out on that nature trail called sin.

Among Christ followers, otherwise known as disciples, I've noticed two different walks. The first shows evidence of the Spirit as the disciple exhibits faith in his or her speech and actions. The second kind of disciple is still trying to *manage* life and is only approachable when things are good. If you identify with Paul, you would agree that doing good requires help! Asking Christ for the strength, mercy, and grace to do good is all part of His will for our lives. God wants us to call on His name to do good. Anything less is a form of trying to control your circumstances and takes glory away from God. There is no Truth in control, and it translates to disobedience to God.

When I capitalize the word *Truth,* it is synonymous with Christ. When there is no Truth in an alleged Christian's life, then that person is considered an antichrist. The Apostle John better explains this in 1 John 4:1–3:

> Dear friends, do not believe every spirit, but test the spirits to see whether they are from God, because many false prophets have gone out into the world. This is how you can recognize the Spirit of God: Every spirit that acknowledges that Jesus Christ has come in the flesh is from God, but every spirit that does not acknowledge Jesus is not from God. This is the spirit of the antichrist, which you have heard is coming and even now is already in the world. (See also 2:22–23)

If you identified with the Christian who is still trying to manage his or her relationship with God, you may consider studying the gospel and epistles of John. Not all who claim to know God have accepted Christ as Lord. I don't know about you, but I have been in conversations with many people who think Christ was a prophet but wholeheartedly deny Him as God in the flesh.

TRAIL TRIALS

The trail we choose determines how we face our trials. There are two trails to choose from, and both are on the opposite extreme: life or death. Chatting about life or death seems a bit harsh at first, but I'd like to broach the subject in this book for those of you who desire to walk on the heels of Christ. If you're still not sure if you want to live all in or all out, please continue because making a final decision really is a matter of life or death!

Now, I wouldn't normally come right out and ask which path you see yourself walking along using those terms as much as I would start asking questions about how you tend to respond to your circumstances. For example, are you more likely to give up on a project that doesn't seem to be going anywhere, or do you continue working at it? When something unexpected happens, are you the type who reacts to the situation, or do you take a deep breath and assess the best way to solve the issue? Involving a friend, someone you're dating, spouse, child, sibling, parent, or co-worker, how do you treat people who don't respond the way you would like them to or perhaps they continually hurt you with their overall behavior? Your answers to each of these questions could get you one step closer to having a right relationship with Christ if you're willing to be honest about your feelings and apply your answers to scripture. Check out Peter's wisdom after hanging out with Jesus for three years:

> For this very reason, make every effort to add to

> your faith goodness; and to goodness, knowledge; and to knowledge, self-control; and to self-control, perseverance; and to perseverance, godliness; and to godliness, brotherly kindness; and to brotherly kindness, love. For if you possess these qualities in increasing measure, they will keep you from being ineffective and unproductive in your knowledge of our Lord Jesus Christ.
>
> 2 Peter 1:5–8

First, you have to have faith in Christ, and then you add a pinch of each of the following ingredients to your life in order to rise like yeast to make daily bread. Getting to know Christ through His Spirit requires us to pursue seven things: goodness, not evil; knowledge, not ignorance; self-control, instead of rage; perseverance, not defeat; godliness, not idolatry (i.e., love of self or money); brotherly kindness, not disrespect; love, not hatred. Are you with me? Because Paul says if God is for us, who can be against us (Romans 8:31)? Believing what these guys have witnessed to us requires tremendous faith on our part. You have to make a daily, if not hourly, commitment to God that you trust in the absolute truth of His Word. I personally pray, "Lord, I am counting on Your promises. I'm completely depending on You to guide and deliver me through this time in my life. Amen!"

Far too often I hear people dismiss their lack of faith in Christ due to a bad experience growing up, while attending a church, or after seeing someone suffer with the loss of a loved one or battle a terminal disease. Did you know that God never promises that we aren't going to suffer? It's the promise of the fall of mankind and that's why we need a Savior to deliver us from evil! Scripture teaches us that the world first hated Jesus, and we are promised that if we choose to follow Him, then we will surely be hated by the world as well (Matthew 10:22, Mark 13:13, Luke 6:22)!

It's time that we all take responsibility for our souls and stop holding sin against a God who hates it. He is holy and perfect; we are the sinners. Why do you think He sacrificed His Son? There are fourteen types of people and actions God hates, and they're all described in the book of Proverbs. Please note that I did not say God hates people but rather the *sin* people commit. For example, Proverbs 3:31 addresses violent people. Other sin includes haughtiness, lying, murdering, stirring up dissension, manipulation, being bent on evil, and pride. Sin comes directly from Satan, and the blame for it should be thrown back on the devil, not God.

CHOOSING YOUR PATH

If not having faith in Christ is the opposite of life, then you are choosing the broader path that leads to certain death. If this statement makes you angry, then please stop reading for a moment and ask yourself why. Remember a few chapters back when I said the proof is in the Bible, not the pudding? We need to study God's Word for ourselves and then make a decision based on what we believe or don't believe about His commands. Jesus uses a parable in Matthew 7:13–14 to aid our decision in trusting in Him: "Enter through the narrow gate. For wide is the gate and broad is the road that leads to destruction, and many enter through it. But small is the gate and narrow the road that leads to life and only a few find it." The narrow gate Jesus is talking about is Him. Salvation through Christ is the only way to Father God, but there are many ways to destruction or death. Another word for death is Hades, and it is mentioned in the Bible five times, four of which are in the book of Revelation. Jesus tells John in a vision in Revelation 1:18, "I am the Living One; I was dead, and behold I am alive for ever and ever! And I hold the keys of death and Hades." In chapter 20, Jesus promises to judge sin and throw death and Hades into a lake of fire, a second death (verses 13–14) for those who reject His salvation.

If you are still angry or can't make yourself believe the Bible in its entirety, then this is probably the path for you. What that means is that everything depends on you while you're physically living, and after you die, your spirit will be eternally separated from God (Revelation 20:15).

A year ago, I had another light-bulb moment when I was talking with a friend who openly asks questions about church and Jesus but never quite gets close enough to making the decision to invite Christ into his heart. It's like a temptation he's resisting because Christ seems to work for me, not him. Sadly, only the devil tempts us. God offered His only Son as a perfect sacrifice to pay our sin debt in full. Salvation through Christ is not a temptation but a gift of grace to deliver us from our nature to sin. The only consequence of living for Christ is the promise of eternal life! For whatever reason, most are willing to acknowledge God but quick to deny Christ as the Son of God and Man.

When tough times come knocking at your door, are you prepared to tap into your faith in Christ for goodness, self-control, knowledge, perseverance, godliness, brotherly kindness, and love, or reach for the usual sinful choices of ignorance, panic, defeat, idolatry, disrespect, and hate?

Walking with God is definitely a full-time job. It requires a commitment to follow His will, faith in Jesus, trust that He is in control of all circumstances, a promise to obey His commands, patience, and a surrendering heart. One of the greatest benefits of choosing this path is that we can stand firm in the midst of any trial and know that we are in the capable hands of the Lord.

FOOTPRINTS

I've begun to say to anyone who will listen that we all have had at least one footprints-in-the-sand (FITS) moment in our lives. My first experience happened when I was hospitalized for three months while doctors tried to figure out why I had a grand mal seizure. During the diagnosis process, I had a near-fatal reaction to an experimental medication. Clinging to life has a major effect on the clinger and the clingees! I have vivid memories of the peace and love I felt as a young child surrounded by my family, church friends, and a kindhearted hospital staff. Jesus was already in my heart at that time, and I felt His arms around me when I could barely lift my head to take a drink of water. For three years after my hospital experience, I was on medication to slow my rapid brain growth, and all that time, Jesus was at the center of my recovery.

Both of my grandmothers died the same year that one of my dogs went off to puppy heaven. Shadow grew up with me and literally was by my side from the time I got up until the time I went to bed at night! She was a Christmas gift the year I got out of the hospital for treatment for my grand mal seizure. My mom says that when she went to pick from the litter, she knew it had to be Shadow because she was in the backyard hunting on the heels of her mom. Shadow was a follower and the cutest Cock-A-Poo Terrier a girl could ever ask for! The spring of my senior year in high school, Shadow mysteriously got sick and died. Searching the house when she failed to meet me at the door after coming home from school one day will forever be etched on my mind. She had walked upstairs and was lying lifeless at the foot of my bed. I was devastated, and a few months later, my grandmother died too; 1988 was a tough year. Exactly twenty years later, my last living grandparent and sweet Cocker Spaniel, Sage Advice, passed away within four months of each other; 2008 was a tough year.

Looking back, there is only one set of footprints for both years. I know you must be saying to yourself, "Sure, it sounds nice to say that, but how can you prove it?" And I'm glad you asked! I have a personal theory that each time I reach my emotional, physical, and spiritual limits, Jesus gives me a breather and lifts me up to God. Leaving home for college in 1988 and being unemployed during 2008 paled in comparison to the losses of my grandparents and dogs in those same years. So the Holy Spirit took over and guided me through the tough times while Jesus delivered me back to wholeness. My losses were gains in drawing near to my Lord and Savior. Each roadblock has been in preparation for the next step in my walk, leaving the impression of Jesus' footprints where mine are absent.

I'm at a point along my nature trail that the glory of the Spirit is like a lamp unto my feet, coaching me around the mud puddles of sin. Like my nephew, I also have a pair of rain boots for added protection for the deeper trials along my trail. I don't always avoid sin because of my fallen nature; however, I do keep my spiritual toolbox close by so I can reach for the necessary faith, surrender, trust, obedience, and patience (S.T.O.P.) when I start to stumble.

It's important to know that God is always present to help you with your next step. It's okay if we slip, stumble, or fall because He has a purpose and plan in every move we make. He uses the tough terrain along our path to grow us spiritually. Proverbs 4:10–12 teaches, "Listen, my son, accept what I say, and the years of your life will be many. I guide you in the way of wisdom and lead you along straight paths. When you walk, your steps will not be hampered; when you run, you will not stumble."

Tears of joy, prayer, praise, and crying out are all part of our outward response to our relationship with

Him, and when you come to a hurdle in the road, be still and know in your heart that Jesus is near to carry you through the forest to safety.

I'm in the midst of my fourth FITS moment, this time as an adult as I start a new career. This may sound unbelievable, but I have enjoyed unemployment and see it as a gift from God. Nearly every day tears of joy well up, burst out, or stream down my cheeks as I celebrate the hope Christ has given me. He is clearly walking me through yet another tough time in my life, and I couldn't be more thankful for the opportunity to dig deeper into my relationship with Him!

I see that He is lovingly using this time to put me face-to-face with some personal and relational sin. Generally, when I'm in the midst of something that forces me out of my comfort zone, I know in my heart that He is trying to get my attention and that change is near. Thankfully, I'm far enough in my walk to stay the course and avoid the pain that comes with turning away from Him. It has been an amazing period of surrendering myself in prayer, and for the first time ever, I have promised that nothing in my life is off limits! Granted, he has been taking me up on my offering, but what's very good about completely trusting God is that I am finally abiding in Him and the body.

Is it hard? Yes. However, Jesus promises that when you and I stick with Him, He will stick with us (John 15:5). Abiding in Christ is another way of saying that He will never leave or forsake us—not now, not ever.

BLUEPRINTS

When I was a kid, my sisters and I used to watch *The Brady Bunch* after school. I liked the episode when the entire family went to Kings Island in Ohio so Mr. Brady could pitch plans to build a new addition at the amusement park. The drama began after Jan mistakenly took his blueprints instead of her Yogi Bear poster! I instantly got a lump in my throat because I knew she was going to get into trouble. To my surprise, the entire bunch got involved and retraced her footsteps until they found the plans that she had accidentally dropped in the middle of a busy street. All was happy and back to normal after Mike was able to meet his five o'clock deadline.

Each of us has a set of blueprints. Your blueprints were drawn up long before they were rolled out at conception. All these years, God has been revealing His plans one day at a time. It's up to you to follow Him in order to redeem all of the blessings He has in store for the rest of your life! Sure, we may get lost or fall along the trail because it's our nature to make mistakes. No one is perfect, and God can use our blunders to grow us spiritually. Hopefully you will learn what I have learned and that is to continually ask God to take you back to the drawing board for redemption through the shed blood of Jesus. There's nothing more powerful than knowing in your heart that you're working with a clean slate.

It's time to consult the blueprint God has for you that details your beginning, middle, and ending. Are you going to walk to the beat of a different drummer, who may look a lot like your*self*, or are you going to follow the drum major, Christ Jesus? If you're not careful, you'll end up where I found myself after fifteen years of building a career—independent and alone. Only when I submitted my rough draft of plans over to God's blueprint did I start to understand and appreciate His attention to detail.

What would you like to see happen during your lifetime? Pray for it and pray big! Keep your spiritual toolbox nearby and start building your own personal relationship with Christ by surrendering, trusting, obeying, and being still while He prepares you for the next phase of your blueprints. Memorize this promise: "For I know the plans I have for you," declares the Lord, "plans to prosper you and not to harm you, plans to give you hope and a future. Then you will call upon me and come and pray to me, and I will listen to you. You will seek me and find me when you seek me with all your heart" (Jeremiah 29:11–13).

Whose footprints are visible along your blueprints? Have you invited Jesus to join you for the rest of your journey? Hopefully by now you are shouting, "Yes!"

I've been talking a lot about making the choice to follow Christ and sharing a handy formula to help you put your focus on Him in all things. Now I'd like to go into more detail of what it means to surrender, trust, obey, have patience, and be faithful to our Lord and Savior. So get your rain boots on and grab a pail and shovel; we have some work to do along our nature trail!

STUDY QUESTIONS

1. To which laws are you bound (see Romans 8:1–2)?

2. What is conquered through Christ?

3. Each day we need to do what?

4. Identify two walks of a believer.

5. Can you honestly say that God has all of your heart?

6. What are the two trails open to *all* creation?

7. Once you've identified your walk (led by Spirit or self) and trail (un/believer), go back to paragraph two of Trail Trials on page 157 and answer all of the questions, plus read 2 Peter 1:5–8 and ask yourself which of these qualities you need in order to make daily bread.

8. Where does the narrow gate described by Jesus in Matthew 7:13–14 lead?

9. Circle one: Is the Bible absolutely true, somewhat true, or not true at all?

10. Do you have any doubt that Christ is the Son of God?

11. What promise do we have in choosing salvation through Christ?

12. What loss has turned out to be a gain in your life?

13. How do you acquire spiritual maturity? (Reread "Footprints")

14. How has God revealed His character in your life?

15. What is off limits to God?

16. Who's the drum major of your blueprints?

17. As of today, are you able to connect the dots of your blueprints?

18. Whose footprints are most visible along your blueprints?

PART FOUR

FAITH AND THE
S.T.O.P. PRINCIPLE

Are faith and trust one in the same? When I share my testimony and talk about having faith in Christ, I also talk about trusting in Him. The way I understand it is that you have to have faith to trust, and when you put the two together, then you're a believer.

The Bible describes faith as reliance, loyalty, or *complete trust* in God or someone else, which are some of the very words (reliance, dependence and hope) the dictionary uses to define trust. So faith and trust are intermingled or dependent upon the other. Trust is a learned behavior and will be outlined in more detail in the pages to follow.

When you accept Christ as Savior, a trade show takes place to spiritually shed your old self for the new (Ephesians 4:22–24). It's like a debutante ball for girls and rite of passage celebration for boys when you buy a fancy outfit and let society know that you are of age, accomplished, and ready for marriage. Once this significant event is over, you spend the rest of your life proving to the world that you have indeed arrived and continue to strive for excellence in your family life, career, and social circles. With salvation, believers take the opportunity to share their testimony of how they were led to accept Christ, pursue a personal relationship, and strive to become more like Him by using their spiritual gifts to build the body of the church.

Confessing your faith in Christ does not guarantee your transformation. It is up to each believer to pursue a relationship that is totally dependent upon His knowledge, strength, and presence. Paul encourages believers, "Do not conform any longer to the pattern of this world, but be transformed by the renewing of your mind. Then you will be able to test and approve what God's will is—his good, pleasing and perfect will" (Romans 12:2). God never forces us to follow Him and has given everyone from Adam and Eve to you and me a free will.

There are always two paths: God's way or yours, and instead of scratching your head and wondering why there are so many facets of having a personal relationship, remember this: we are never asked to do something Christ hasn't already accomplished before us. If following His teachings and commands lead to becoming more Christlike we are all the more pleasing to God.

"And we, who with unveiled faces all reflect the Lord's glory, are being transformed into his likeness with ever-increasing glory, which comes from the Lord, who is the Spirit" (2 Corinthians 3:18).

One day, before Jesus was crucified, He took Peter, James, and John with him to the top of a mountain. It was there that all His glory was revealed and the three disciples learned His identity and power as the Son of God (see Matthew 17:2; Mark 9:2; Luke 9:28). "A voice came from the cloud, saying, 'This is my Son, whom I have chosen; listen to him'" (Luke 9:35). Jesus was left standing alone after Moses and Elijah had left the mountain to confirm Jesus' identity in God as His Son, just as we are identified in Christ upon salvation as His child.

Transformation happens when you choose the Spirit over your way of doing things. It's that light-bulb moment when you make the connection that living in the Spirit means you're not living for self or the world. You're bent on God, not sinfulness, just as Jesus fulfilled all God had laid out for Him to do up to that point on the mountainside.

Faith requires trust. You need to decide if you believe that God is the Creator of the world you live in and whether or not Jesus did in fact die on the cross offering salvation. If you put your trust in God that His promises in the Bible are true and profess faith in Jesus, then you are saved by His grace. If you only believe in God and think Jesus was a good guy who lived and died like the rest of us will someday, then you are not saved or reconciled to God.

By our faith in Jesus, we are acknowledging that we are sinners and that God sent the perfect sacrifice, His

Son, to wipe away all our sin, to cleanse us (sanctify) in preparation to reside with God in heaven after our physical death. But here are two of many verses that seem to trip unbelievers up and may be at the root of contention for you too:

> Jesus answered, "I am the way and the truth and the life. No one comes to the Father except through me."
>
> John 14:6

> Now to you who believe, this stone is precious. But to those who do not believe, "The stone the builders rejected has become the capstone," and, "A stone that causes men to stumble and a rock that makes them fall." They stumble because they disobey the message—which is also what they were destined for.
>
> 1 Peter 2:7–8

Please don't choose to stumble any longer and accept Jesus into your heart today!

If you already have committed your life to Jesus, you are saved by the grace of God; no one can take away your salvation (John 6:39). You have the rest of your life to build a personal relationship with Christ through His Spirit who now dwells in you. Stop living according to your old self and start anew by following the S.T.O.P. principle. It will help equip you with the necessary spiritual tools for a successful relationship with our Savior:

☐ Surrender

☐ Trust

☐ Obedience

☐ Patience

SURRENDER

If surrender were easy, we would all be in line with God's will for our lives. It takes great effort to give what you want up to God in prayer and to leave it there. For most, surrender is confused with taking control and leads to more loose ends and frustration.

Benjamin Franklin once said, "God helps those who help themselves." Americans, including Christians, have been erroneously using his misleading statement for Scripture to accomplish their goals on their terms. Consequently, God is nowhere to be found in the midst of a personal trial because of the philosophical words of one man who happens to be a founding father of this great country. Ben may have had an electric personality and wit, but he cannot light your path like the saving grace of Jesus Christ!

Surrender is a process. It seems like every day there is an addition to the trial I am facing, and I'm convinced it's God's way of reminding me that (a) He will see me through the trial when I solely focus on Him, and (b) others will not be able to mistake delivery of said trial by my own effort but by His hand. That's how God revealed His character to the world before Christ arrived on the scene. He spoke to those who had faith in Him, like Noah, Abraham, and Moses, and helped them lead His people out of bondage to freedom. Without complete surrender in Christ, you will always be in bondage to sin.

How do you know that you've completely surrendered? First, you have to ask yourself if doing things your way has gotten you the desired result. If yes, then you will most likely scoff at the idea of trusting God to lead your life. If you've come to the end of self and finally see that all of your efforts to handle a situation have failed, then you have been humbled and may be ready for the next step.

There have been many times when I *thought* I had relinquished control over to God until I caught myself helping myself. Remember that Satan does not want you, under any circumstances, to give control of your life up to God. So he will deceive you in any way he knows how to get you to stumble and fall. A common trap I have observed, especially with high unemployment numbers looming, is how people identify their entire value according to their profession. All self-esteem, power, and (many times, abuse of) control come from doing and keeping their job. If this is you, you are in major bondage, and the devil has you right where he needs and wants you to stay! You are in grave spiritual danger, and the only way out from under it is by calling on the name of Jesus.

In John 15:2, Jesus says, "While every branch that does bear fruit he prunes so that it will be even more fruitful." What that means is that God may discipline us by taking the pruning shears to our branches (a.k.a.

excruciating trials), but He does it with great love and care so that we may blossom spiritually and grow closer to Him in the vine.

In a season, the branches that have been methodically selected for pruning have taken off and sprouted new growth. All pain is forgotten as we flourish in God's glory; however, disease can set in and take us over in the midst of our new growth. Satan is the master of using our struggles against us. You may have noticed during your trials that the moment God clips the last branch and you're experiencing a lot of pain, Satan is right there to tempt you and tries to discourage you from praying for deliverance. When this happens—and write this down, please—get on your knees and ask God to grant you peace. Pray for the gift of peace for as long as you're in step with His will. *Peace is the compass to the hope we have in Christ.* It will see you through the toughest of times. If you fall into Satan's trap and quit the surrendering process, God will discipline until you get your focus back on Him, not your painful circumstances.

If you're experiencing doubt, anxiety, or guilt, it is not of God but rather Satan. Confusion, smoke, and mirrors are all a part of Satan's subtle tactics to get your eyes off God and onto your circumstances. When you have a bad feeling and your gut has your attention, treat it as a God-given wakeup call to get your focus back on Him! Outside of trusting Christ as Savior, you will never have true peace.

Third, come to terms with the fact that the more you give control of your life up to God, the more Satan will attack you. As you see God working, surrendering your will to Christ will become a larger part of your prayer life, and your peace level will also rise. Naturally, Satan isn't going to be happy about your increased obedience, so make sure you're paying attention to your feelings and are correctly identifying its source. Surrender is a choice, not a feeling, but emotions like fear and doubt are indicative of Satan attacking your right choice to follow God's will. Look at it this way: the opposite of chaos and control is surrender because you're willing to trade in the old self or familiar way of living for the blessings God has in store for your life (Ephesians 4:22–24).

Surrender is change in the works and the act of giving up in favor of another (The American Heritage Dictionary of the English Language, third edition n.d.). It will require tremendous faith that God's way is the best course of action and a commitment on your part to pray each time you feel yourself twitching to help yourself again! Also, you cannot fully experience God's will for your life without surrender. Once you have faith in Christ, surrender is the necessary act of getting the focus off you and others so God can reveal His plan and purpose. You have two choices of either trying to control your own circumstances or knowing that God is in control of all circumstances and that His plan is right for you. Remember, if there's no peace, then Christ is not at the center of your life.

I honestly know in my heart when I'm doing things my way or God's because of how I feel inside. It's like I have an internal alarm clock that goes off each time

I take one step away from the center of His will. I've come to depend on my compass o' peace and know that I will soon see the change He is bringing to light for my life. I've also learned to welcome trials and am honored that Jesus is knocking at my door. Jesus will always pursue you too, and it's your choice to respond by surrendering or by continuing in the abyss you currently call life.

God does not help those who help themselves. God helps those who call on His name and surrender their will to His. Pray for peace as your compass. Surrender each and every time you experience doubt, fear, anxiety, or anything that is not of God. Then wait on the Lord to reveal His perfect and complete plan for your life. He will take your surrender and deliver you *every* time; it's His promise!

Oh, and if you think that you're surrendering and you're not at peace, then God is pursuing you, and He is preparing you for a change or two. Please accept His prompting and lay out your life before Him. Promise that nothing is off limits even if you think that you're living in accordance to His will. You are not at peace for a reason, so trust God to show you why.

Surrender is such a difficult yet essential act to apply in your walk and is rewarding when you do. Here are five references that will help you study surrender in your life:

> Teach me to do your will, for you are my God;
> may your good Spirit lead me on level ground.
>
> Psalm 143:10

Then Jesus said to his disciples, "If anyone would come after me, he must deny himself and take up his cross and follow me. For whoever wants to save his life will lose it, but whoever loses his life for me will find it."

Matthew 16:24–25

If you remain in me and my words remain in you, ask whatever you wish, and it will be given you.

John 15:7

Those who live according to the sinful nature have their minds set on what that nature desires; but those who live in accordance with the Spirit have their minds set on what the Spirit desires.

Romans 8:5

Those controlled by the sinful nature cannot please God.

Romans 8:8

- ☑ Surrender
- ☐ Trust
- ☐ Obedience
- ☐ Patience

Trust

Trust is a learned behavior and is the "firm reliance on the integrity, ability, or character of a person or thing. One in which confidence is placed. To have or place reliance, depend, hope" (The American Heritage Dictionary of the English Language, third edition n.d.). A few key words that pop out from this definition include *character, depend,* and *hope.*

Learning to trust is the second of five helpful tools in building a personal relationship with Christ. It is close in nature to patience and requires a great deal of surrender through prayer. Each time God answers you, you will find yourself trusting a little more, as well as getting a glimpse of His character. God promises we all have a plan and purpose (Jeremiah 29:11), He promises He will never abandon us (Deuteronomy 31:6), and He sacrificed His Son to fulfill His Word (John 3:16). Romans 5:3–5 confirms, "Not only so, but we also rejoice in our sufferings, because we know that suffering produces perseverance; perseverance, character; and character, hope. And hope does not disappoint us, because God has poured out his love into our hearts by the Holy Spirit, whom he has given us."

We have hope in Christ because of what He did at the cross. It conquers the hopelessness we feel when we do wrong and have no way of reconciling on our own merit. Hope is an intangible promise of God that we are His creation, which He wants to rid us of our sin nature and replace it with His Spirit through faith in Christ.

"For in this hope we were saved. But hope that is

seen is no hope at all. Who hopes for what he already has? But if we hope for what we do not yet have, we wait for it patiently" (Romans 8:24–25).

At one time, false prophets went around telling believers that only a chosen few were privy to the knowledge of God, but in a letter to the Colossian church, Paul said, "To them God has chosen to make known among the Gentiles the glorious riches of this mystery, which is Christ in you, the hope of glory" (Colossians 1:27). So he clears up the so-called secret plan of God by revealing it is Christ living in us, and we all have equal access to His glory if we so choose to follow Him.

Trust is also synonymous to our faith in Christ. After you personally choose to step out in faith by believing that Christ is who He claims to be, then you begin trusting the absolute truth of the Bible. In 1 Corinthians 13:13, Paul explains, "And now these three remain: faith, hope and love. But the greatest of these is love." Just before this fabulous verse he explains that love is patient and kind, it also rejoices with the truth, always protects, *trusts, hopes,* and perseveres (verses 4–7)! None of us could have said it better. When you love someone, you put your hope and trust in him or her. You grow the relationship through the good times and bad. You also protect who and what you've come to love with all your strength. This is the role Christ assumes when we trust in Him.

There's a certain level of dependency when we trust in others, but total dependence if we truly pursue the kind of relationship Christ offers. Once saved, you have admitted that you can no longer do things on your own and completely depend upon His love, forgiveness, and guidance.

It's funny, but the more I try to explain the S.T.O.P. principle, the more clear it becomes that each tool needs to constantly be working together to build our faith. We must daily surrender control of our circumstances to Him, trust that He has a purpose, obey His plan, and be patient, respecting His timing, not our own.

The best first step in trusting in the Lord is to pray for wisdom and strength as He begins to work on changing your heart and mind. If you don't allow Christ to work *in* you, the Holy Spirit will never be revealed to others *through* you. Tell Jesus that you trust Him and surrender any uneasy feelings or thoughts to Him. He wants you to trust Him and can only accomplish so much without it. As Proverbs 3:5 wisely advises, "Trust in the Lord with all your heart and lean not on your own understanding."

Satan wants you to depend upon your finite understanding. Choose to deny Satan. You can trust God!

> But I trust in you, O Lord; I say, "You are my God."
>
> Psalm 31:14

> I will save you; you will not fall by the sword but will escape with your life, because you trust in me, declares the Lord.
>
> Jeremiah 39:18

> The Lord is good, a refuge in times of trouble. He cares for those who trust in him.
>
> Nahum 1:7

"Do not let your hearts be troubled. Trust in God; trust also in me."

John 14:1

And again, "I will put my trust in him."

Hebrews 2:13

☑ Surrender
☑ Trust
☐ Obedience
☐ Patience

OBEY

Jesus is the most obedient person you will ever know. Jesus defines the word *obedience* with His life, death, resurrection, and promise to return to claim all believers as His own. The disciple John tells us, "In the beginning was the Word, and the Word was with God, and the Word was God. He (Jesus; see verse 14) was with God in the beginning" (John 1:1–2). These verses establish Jesus' divinity and identity as God in the flesh. Throughout the book of John, we learn through Jesus' testimony that God's plan for His life on earth was to instruct and save us from condemnation. It took complete surrender, obedience, and trust to follow through with this plan, and only Jesus, the perfect sacrifice, could do it for us.

For as much as I love music, I'm lyrically challenged

but not when it comes to childhood hymns like "Jesus Loves Me" and "Amazing Grace." I also love the hymn "Trust and Obey" by Daniel B. Towner and John H. Sammis. It will often silence me as I ponder the magnitude of the words:

> When we walk with the Lord in the light of His Word,
> What a glory He sheds on our way!
> While we do His good will, He abides with us still,
> And with all who will trust and obey
>
> Refrain:
> Trust and obey, for there's no other way
> To be happy in Jesus, but to trust and obey.
>
> Not a shadow can rise, not a cloud in the skies,
> But His smile quickly drives it away;
> Not a doubt or a fear, not a sigh or a tear,
> Can abide while we trust and obey.
>
> Not a burden we bear, not a sorrow we share,
> But our toil He doth richly repay;
> Not a grief or a loss, not a frown or a cross,
> But is blessed if we trust and obey.
>
> But we never can prove the delights of His love
> Until all on the altar we lay;
> For the favor He shows, for the joy He bestows,
> Are for them who will trust and obey.

Then in fellowship sweet we will sit at His feet,
Or we'll walk by His side in the way;
What He says we will do, where He sends we will
go;
Never fear, only trust and obey.
(Towner and Sammis 1887)

How often do I truly trust in the Lord for all things and without question obey Him when He taps me on the shoulder to do something that will take me in the opposite direction of where I'm headed? Until recently, not very often, was the answer. Obedience fights our fallen nature, and if you don't surrender control of your life to God each day, sin can overrule every decision you make.

I believe there are a couple of ways we come to obey Christ. First is what I call an obedience meat sandwich! In this instance, we trust in God as He leads us to do something that is out of our league, choose to obey His call, and then trust in His deliverance. So obedience is the meat between two pieces of toasted (or untoasted) trust bread. A second way of obeying Christ requires a switch-a-roo of the lyrics we sing, "Trust and obey, for there's no other way" because it's our obedience to Christ that often precedes our trust. We automatically obey God's Word *before* we think to trust in His promises of strength, mercy, courage, etc., to get us through the trial at hand. The latter is one way of knowing that you have been transformed in your walk with Christ.

Over and over again we are taught in the Bible that God does not ask us to say or do anything (1) that He has not equipped us for (1 Corinthians 10:13) and that (2) Jesus didn't already accomplish ahead of us (John 17:4; 19:28).

The more you study Scripture, the more you will learn how to surrender, trust, and obey God.

I became transformed in my thinking and relationship with Christ when I truly understood surrender. During two separate trials, God made it clear to me that nothing in my life depends on me or on anyone else. Everything depends on Him! It was at that very moment that the veil of darkness was lifted from my eyes and I was able to see my disobedience and hand over *all* control to God. I was immediately transformed, and the burden of self was no longer mine! Like faith, I had a choice to make about who is responsible for my life. The first step for all believers is to accept Christ as Lord of all. Another essential step involves choosing obedience to His will, not yours or anyone else's!

The most awe-inspiring example of obedience is when Jesus prayed before his arrest and crucifixion in Matthew 26:39: "My Father, if it is possible, may this cup be taken from me. Yet not as I will, but as you will." The Bible says Jesus was so overcome with sorrow for the sin that was about to separate Him from God that He asked if it was God's will to take it away. Notice Jesus followed His petition with "but as you will," knowing that His obedience to God's will was the only way to glorify God and bring hope to the world by paying the price for our sins with His life. Jesus conquered death as God raised Him from the grave, and we are promised the same (1 Corinthians 6:14). The Holy Spirit is in all believers and has the power to raise us from the dead at Christ's return. How cool is that?

Your automatic act of obedience in any issue will reap the fruit of the Spirit, like love, joy, peace, patience, kindness, goodness, faithfulness, gentleness, and self-control (Galatians 5:22–23). Ask the Holy Spirit to guide you in all things and pray for His fruit in your life. It can only come from knowing Jesus personally. Obedience leads to transformation in your relationship with Christ and shares the bond of love that unites the Father and Son.

> But I gave them this command: Obey me, and I will be your God and you will be my people. Walk in all the ways I command you, that it may go well with you.
>
> Jeremiah 7:23

> Whoever has my commands and obeys them, he is the one who loves me. He who loves me will be loved by my Father, and I too will love him and show myself to him.
>
> John 14:21

> Peter and the other apostles replied: "We must obey God rather than men!"
>
> Acts 5:29

> And being found in appearance as a man, he humbled himself and became obedient to death—even death on a cross!
>
> Philippians 2:8

> Although he was a son, he learned obedience from what he suffered and, once made perfect, he became the source of eternal salvation for all who obey him.
>
> Hebrews 5:8–9

☑ Surrender

☑ Trust

☑ Obedience

☐ Patience

PATIENCE

Like all of the other tools that are necessary to properly build a personal relationship with Christ so is our need for patience. You'll need to keep it close to your heart because patience always follows an act of obedience! Getting back to the obedience meat sandwich model, patience is the condiment that completes your tasty deli delight.

If you're trying to cut back and save some calories, you may try to skip the condiments, but when we're talking about our walk with God, you will need to make sure you spread a generous amount of patience on both pieces of trust bread. Exercising or dismissing patience could mean the deliverance or destruction of God's plan for your life.

There are countless examples of people God chose to complete His will, including Noah, Moses, and Esther that involved tremendous faith and patience. In Esther 4:14–16, we learn:

> "For if you remain silent at this time, relief and deliverance for the Jews will arise from another place, but you and your father's family will perish. And who knows but that you have come to royal position for such a time as this?" Then Esther sent

this reply to Mordecai: "Go, gather together all the Jews who are in Susa, and fast for me. Do not eat or drink for three days, night or day. I and my maids will fast as you do. When this is done, I will go to the king, even though it is against the law. And if I perish, I perish."

Esther was an attractive Jewish woman who won the favor of King Xerxes of Persia. As queen, she was still not allowed to approach the king unless she was summoned, so she asked her cousin Mordecai and her people to fast and pray with her for a period of three days and nights. Patience became key for the deliverance of the Jews, who were to be slaughtered in a plot by the king's wicked right-hand man, Haman. The story ends with Haman being publicly hung at the same gallows he built to use on Mordecai and others who would not submissively bow to him.

Not only did Esther exhibit a tremendous amount of faith, but she also showed great wisdom in choosing first to fast and pray (surrender circumstances), trust, obey those in authority over her, and patiently wait for an answer from God. I want to respond to all things in my life like Esther did, and the best way to understand patience in your walk is to know that it is the lifeline to deliverance. Without quietly, patiently waiting upon the Lord for direction, you will make poor choices and fail every time. Patience requires us to be still and to listen for God's answers.

One way to pass the time in between obedience and deliverance is to get into the Word and read how others handled their downtime. Not to get off track, but I often wondered if Jonah spent his quiet time inside the great fish that swallowed him plugging his nose! If you notice his story, Jonah lived inside the fish for three days and three nights (Jonah 1:17). In the New Testament, Jesus refers to Jonah's story to prove His authority over death within three days and three nights (Matthew 12:39–41; 16:4). Again, how cool is that? Patience means something to God. He doesn't leave us out to dry until he gets around to answering our prayers and petitions. His Word says he is either busy working behind the scenes or working *in* us to make the necessary heart changes so He can work *through* us to accomplish His will! Amen?

God has faithfully delivered me from the hands of the devil each time I *surrendered* complete control of my circumstances, *trusted* His purpose for the trial, *obeyed* His call to follow Him, and then *patiently waited* for Him to bring me through to the other side. Being still is not a natural tendency, but it becomes a part of your life the more you surrender your old ways to Him. It comforts you and allows the Holy Spirit to counsel, or lift you up in your greatest time of need. Here are a few verses that teach us the importance of quiet time with God:

> Wait for the Lord; be strong and take heart and wait for the Lord.
>
> Psalm 27:14

> The end of a matter is better than its beginning, and patience is better than pride. Do not be quickly provoked in your spirit, for anger resides in the lap of fools.
>
> Ecclesiastes 7:8–9

This is what the Sovereign Lord, the Holy One of Israel, says: "In repentance and rest is your salvation, in quietness and trust is your strength, but you would have none of it." Yet the Lord longs to be gracious to you; he rises to show you compassion. For the Lord is a God of justice. Blessed are all who wait for him!

Isaiah 30:15, 18

But those who hope in the Lord will renew their strength. They will soar on wings like eagles; they will run and not grow weary, they will walk and not be faint.

Isaiah 40:31

I say to myself, "The Lord is my portion; therefore I will wait for him"...it is good to wait quietly for the salvation of the Lord. Let him sit alone in silence, for the Lord has laid it on him.

Lamentations 3:24, 26, and 28

Because you know that the testing of your faith develops perseverance. Perseverance must finish its work so that you may be mature and complete, not lacking anything.

James 1:3–4

When you learn to patiently listen for God's direction, counsel, and forgiveness, you will be able to hear and know each time you are obediently walking in His will. If it seems as though He's not answering, go back to surrendering your circumstances to Him, followed by the other three principles. God's silence can sometimes be a test of will with the goal to build a deeper trust system. Remember when I mentioned I could hear crickets during my syndication trial? Crickets are your friends when it comes to breaking the silence, plus a reminder that God is all around you! Step out in faith, be quiet, and stand firm, okay? He promises deliverance; you have His Word!

- ☑ Surrender
- ☑ Trust
- ☑ Obedience
- ☑ Patience

STUDY QUESTIONS

1. Define *faith* in Christ.

2. What is old and new in your testimony?

3. Who has free will?

4. When are believers transformed?

5. List three things faith requires.

6. What does faith in Christ proclaim?

7. The S.T.O.P. principle is an acronym for what?

SURRENDER

1. What is the opposite of surrender?

2. To rid myself of ugly sin, I first need to:

3. Pruning is synonymous to the trials in our lives. What does it accomplish?

4. What does peace accomplish?

5. Circle one: Surrender is a choice or a feeling. What does it do?

6. Who does God help?

7. What should you do if you think you're surrendering and there's no peace?

TRUST

1. What do surrender and trust have in common?

2. When/why is suffering good?

3. Define hope.

4. What is the mystery of God? (See Colossians 1:27 and 2:2)

5. Why are trust and faith in Christ synonymous?

6. Total dependence upon Christ requires _____ and develops _____.

7. Do you fully trust God or do you need more answers? How much more understanding do you need before you do trust Him?

OBEY

1. Who set the example of how to obey God?

2. How did this person do it?

3. What are the ingredients of an OMS (obedient meat sandwich)?

4. Does God ask us to do the impossible (reread 1 Corinthians 10:13; John 17:4 and 19:28; also Luke 18:27; Matthew 19:26)?

5. Who will resurrect all sinners who claim Christ as Savior?

6. List a few of the fruits of obedience.

PATIENCE

1. What does patience follow?

2. If obedience and trust make the sandwich, then what adds flavor?

3. How did Esther handle conflict (see Esther 4:16)?

4. How did God respond (study Esther 5:2–4 and 8:11–13)?

5. Discuss a couple of ways you can wisely use your spare time.

6. In between answered prayer, what are some things God is doing for patient believers?

7. What can you do if you feel God has *not* heard your prayers?

8. Is there a step we must take in order for our faith to increase?

CONCLUSION

WALKING SHOES FIT FOR A NARROW PATH!

Wearing in a new pair of shoes can be a really painful process. Add choosing to follow Christ along the winding path of righteousness and you undoubtedly have a few hurdles ahead of you! What I have come to learn and desire in my heart is a stronger, more faithful relationship with the Perfect One who lovingly lighted the same path I have since chosen to tread in my life.

Imagine the greatness of that statement; Jesus has already walked the narrow path to make way for those who believe in His name. He has cleared away our debt to sin by leaving a trail of broken bread and fountain of living water so we may never hunger, thirst, or be lost but found in Him.

Please pursue the S.T.O.P. principle one tool at a time. Surrender is perhaps one of the hardest to learn. Like practicing an instrument for a recital, you have to continually rehearse until you finally get it. My sister and I spent many years trying to understand and apply what it means to give *all* control over to God. Each one of us seems to be so immersed in self and/or our circumstances that it's truly a daily, if not hourly, struggle to fully let go. If you find yourself holding on to just a remnant of control, you will never have the peace God rewards those believers who do obey and trust that He has the best plan.

Make patience a priority. Take time in your daily routine to quietly be with the Lord in prayer and read the Bible. Where do you start? Choose a book that you have never studied before and pray before you start reading that God reveal something new. You will find that the more you spend time feeding your spiritual needs, the more patient *and* efficient you become!

Shop around for the right shoes for you. If you decide to step into the pair Christ has already paid the price, your feet will be protected with the gospel of peace (Ephesians 6:15) for the remainder of your earthly journey.

Someday I hope you welcome each trial along your trail with the promise in your heart that Jesus loved us first and is waiting with open arms at the end of the path to raise us into heaven for an eternity with YHWH.

STUDY QUESTIONS

1. Who leads the narrow path?

2. What did He leave in His wake?

3. You forfeit _____ when you try to control your circumstances.

4. What exercises will help you learn patience?

5. Who has paid the price for your shoes?

6. Share with your group the path you have chosen and how you plan to stay on course.

FAITH AND THE S.T.O.P. PRINCIPLE

STUDY GUIDE ANSWER KEY

I'M IN CONTROL

1. During any given day, do you feel more in or out of control of your life? Answers will vary.

2. If everything depends on you, then whom do you trust in your darkest hour? Answers will vary.

3. According to Romans 8:28, those who love God also have a God-given purpose. What is yours? Answers will vary.

4. Have you ever had a time in your life when you tried to hide from God? Were you successful? Answers will vary.

5. Only one question in our lifetime has eternal value attached to the answer. What is the question we must all answer? A: Do I believe that Christ is fully God, fully man, and the risen Savior of mankind?

6. How have you pursued *relating* to Christ? Answers will vary.

7. What three things happen when you put your focus on Christ? A: (1) A transition from trying to control your circumstances to recognizing all things go through Him first. (2) Surrendering said control over to Him each and every day and (3) a *desire* to change to be more like Him.

8. Is *living for* Christ the same as *accepting* Christ as Savior? A: Each person must decide if he or she is a sinner in need of redemption through the shed blood of Jesus Christ. If yes, then he or she needs to accept Him as Savior. Living for Christ does not imply being born again.

9. What does transformation mean? A: Transformation means complete dependence upon the Lord by putting Christ at the center of all things, not self.

10. If God is on your shelf, who or what are you giving priority? Answers will vary.

11. What is required of you to ask Christ to be your personal Savior? A: A decision to let go of your former way of living and asking Christ into your heart as Lord and Savior of your life.

12. Describe what happens to your heart once you choose Christ. A: The Holy Spirit guides and counsels while indwelling each believer.

13. Define surrender. A: To give up in favor of another. It is our faith in Christ that teaches us complete surrender. First, we must profess our faith in Christ. Surrender requires believers to give complete control of their lives to Christ.

14. What is the opposite of faith? A: Control

15. Why was Jesus crucified? A: Jesus was crucified for His unconditional love for us. We are all fallen and

need a Savior to redeem us so we may be purified in order to go before God in heaven. Christ died in our place so we may live with the Father in heaven should we accept His atonement for our sins.

16. Have man-made rules paved your path to relationship or rebellion? Answers will vary.

17. What do you think will happen if you decide to completely depend on Christ? Answers will vary.

WHO I AM

1. List at least one item you can praise God for each day. Answers will vary.

2. According to Colossians 2:13–17, what was nailed to the cross with Christ? A: In Christ we are no longer bound to the ceremonial and civil laws; however, we do continue to follow the Ten Commandments.

3. Define grace. A: God's free and unmerited favor for sinful humanity.

4. What are you acquiring? Answers will vary.

5. List your current top five priorities. Answers will vary.

6. Is spending time in the Word anywhere on your list? Answers will vary.

7. When have you asked yourself, "Is this it?" A: Answers will vary.

8. True or false: Righteousness = Truth = Christ = eternal life. True

9. How did the Apostle Paul answer the "Is this it" question? A: Living *in* sin leads to death and being set free *from* sin through Christ leads to eternal life!

THE KINGDOM OF ME

1. Where does the phrase "the writing is on the wall" originate? A: Daniel 5:5

2. Who or what is at the *center* of your attention? Answers will vary.

3. How have you tried and failed to get up close and personal with God? Answers will vary.

4. What rules or past sin(s) are holding you back from growing in the love of Christ? Answers will vary.

5. Does fear motivate the decisions you make or do you go to Christ first? Answers will vary.

6. Do you believe you can depend on Christ for *all* things? A: Yes (hopefully)!

7. True or false: Control = sin = bondage = Satan. True

8. Referring back to your current top five priorities (review chapter 2), give an overview of the first one on your list. Is it still number one? Answers will vary.

9. Is God trying to get your attention? If so, how? Answers will vary.

10. Human (sin) nature dictates that we look within ourselves for all the answers. What idols are keeping you from putting Christ first? Answers may include

but are not limited to: money, control, weight, kids, spouse, sex, and job.

11. What do you have to have that is worth forfeiting what God has to give? Answers will vary.

12. Is the writing on the wall regarding your spiritual life? Answers will vary.

13. What do you think the ancient fingers of Daniel would write on your heart today? Answers will vary.

14. Do you struggle with how God would truly love you? Explain why or why not. Answers will vary.

SHELF THE SELF

1. Are you willing to give up and walk away from God for good or would you like to learn how to be renewed in His Spirit? Answer is intended to draw out why believers tend to focus on other things and people than God, therefore straying and/or blaming God for worldly sin. Choosing renewal in the Spirit will require a focus adjustment and heart change.

2. Spend each day this week journaling about your past and present circumstances. Scripture teaches that nothing comes to you before going through Him. The day before your group meets, spend intimate time with God and pray for Him to quiet you with His love. If you've never petitioned His love before, simply pray Zephaniah 3:17, plus read from your journal. Listen. What do you hear?

TRADING CENTERS

1. Describe a time of struggle and strain in your life. Answers will vary.

2. Has God ever answered your prayer in the last hour? What was the outcome? Answers will vary.

3. At what point has your walk with God shown evidence of spiritual growth? Answers should reflect transformation point in a believer's walk.

4. Is there a difference between success and God's blessing? Answers will vary. I was able to discern God's blessing from personal success when I realized He was equipping me for ministry within my workplace by providing high ratings that provided job security.

5. What is the ministry God has planned for you? Answers will vary.

6. Has God ever prompted a change of heart in your career goals, family, or other area of your life? Answers will vary.

7. Are you more prone to worry or trust God when times get tough? Answer is intended to prompt believer to denounce worry as sin and of Satan, not from God.

8. What is your source for peace? A: Peace is freedom from strife or discord and can only come from God.

9. Is it possible to have peace outside of God? A: Worldly peace is not the same as the peace we receive from the Spirit and is only temporary.

10. Do you know the peace, joy, and contentment Christ promises in the midst of all circumstances? Answers will vary.

3D

1. List your spiritual gift(s). Answers will vary.

2. Are you guilty of trying to define God? A: In the second commandment, God forbids us to make an idol in His image (Exodus 20: 4–6). What that means is that we all try at some point to get our minds around God and we go to great lengths to bring Him to our spiritual level of understanding. We often want to contain God so we can manage our relationship with Him.

3. Why or why not do you believe in a 3-D God? Answers will vary.

4. Outside of God speaking to His believers, what are some other ways He communicates with us? A: Touch, smell, taste, and sight.

5. In 2 Corinthians 2:15–16, Paul says we are *the aroma of Christ* to God. To whom are we the *smell of death?* A: The aroma was sweet to the winners and the smell of death to the losers.

6. Share a time God has touched your life. Answers will vary.

7. Who has seen God and how do we see Him today? A: No one except Jesus, who is in the image of God, has seen God. The Apostle John who lived with Jesus tells us, "The Word became flesh and made his dwelling among us. We have seen his glory, the glory of the One and Only, who came from the Father, full of grace and truth" (John 1:14). We see God in Creation and Christ in us.

8. What have or are you trying to conceal from God? Answers will vary.

9. How can we utilize our sense of taste in relation to God? A: During the Last Supper, "Jesus took bread, gave thanks and broke it, and gave it to his disciples, saying, 'Take and eat; this is my body'" (Matthew 26:26). Today, believers eat bread in remembrance of Him during communion. Bread is a symbol of Christ's atoning body. A second way we taste is through God's Word.

10. What resource is available to all who seek the opportunity to touch, see, taste, smell and hear God? A: God's Word, the Bible, Christ in the flesh, Truth.

I AM

1. Do you believe Jesus is the Son of God? Answers may vary.

2. What does God desire to have with *all* His creation? A: God loves us unconditionally and wants to be in a relationship with us, and He sent His Son to do it.

3. Where is God when you're trying to avoid Him? A: He's omnipresent; you can't escape His presence!

4. When have you claimed God's glory for your own? Answers will vary.

5. What promise are we given in Romans 8:26–27? A: "In the same way, the Spirit helps us in our weakness. We do not know what we ought to pray for, but the Spirit himself intercedes for us with groans that words cannot express. And he who searches our hearts knows the mind of the Spirit, because the Spirit intercedes for the saints (believers) in accordance with God's will."

6. Do you face any impossibilities? Answers will vary.

Are you ready to put your complete faith in Christ? If so, please pray:

> Dear heavenly Father, I come to you as a sinner in need of a Savior. I confess my sin and ask that the shed blood of Jesus cleanse me of all wrongdoing and that I may live out the rest of my life according to Your perfect will, not my own. I believe Christ died so I may have eternal life by believing in His Holy name. Please come into my heart, Lord Jesus. Amen!

7. Society pushes the mantra, "Trust no one but yourself." Do you agree or disagree? Answers will vary.

8. List the two forms of obedience. A: Voluntary or involuntary.

9. What tool will help you to choose obedience over sin? A: The best tool for obedience is trusting Jesus; neither can succeed without the other.

10. How is trust challenged? A: Patience and quiet time! Listen for the Lord to speak. Waiting around for answers is one of the most difficult aspects of the Christian life and requires tremendous faith.

11. When has God patiently waited upon you? Answers will vary.

12. When have you patiently waited upon God? What was the outcome? Answers will vary.

13. There is One Way to God, but many ways to Christ. What is your testimony? Testimonies will vary!

US

1. In Hebrew, *toledôth* means a subsequent or emergent account of something previously described or explained. How do Genesis chapters one and two compliment the other? A: While Genesis 1 gives us an *overview* of how the universe was created, Genesis 2:4–25 gives us further *insight* as to how man was created.

2. On a scale of one to ten, are you more isolated, balanced, or social? Answers will vary.

3. How do you fill the void in your life (who or what)? Answers will vary.

4. If you were to peel away all the layers of business

associates, neighbors, and acquaintances, whom would you find in your community? Answers will vary.

5. Would you agree or disagree that you value being by yourself more than committing to others? Why? Answers will vary.

6. Find Scripture that instructs *us* how to relate to one another in community. (For example, 1 Corinthians 12:12–31) A: Also Galatians 2:20, Ephesians 3:6, etc.

7. Describe how you know you are in a true relationship with God, Christ, and the Holy Spirit. A: I am never alone or apart from Him. Jesus is in me and I in Him (John 15:5).

8. Comparing the fruits of the Spirit and the acts of the sin nature outlined in Galatians 5, what sin do you need to switch out to only bear fruit? A: Jealousy, fits of rage, selfish ambition, etc.

9. How do we know God hears our prayers? A: Jesus promises us in Matthew 18:19–20, "Again, I tell you that if two of you on earth agree about anything you ask for, it will be done for you by my Father in heaven. For where two or three come together in my name, there am I with them."

10. List one benefit of being in community with other believers. A: Being held accountable; considering someone else's needs, thoughts or feelings.

11. When has God shown up during your prayers? Answers will vary.

12. Have you ever tried to force God to work for you by demanding certain results? Answers will vary.

13. List any frustration with your prayer life. Answers will vary.

14. Discuss ways you can change how you pray and listen for God to answer. Answers will vary and may include praying for God to prepare your heart to accept His will.

15. Who should believers initially go to for guidance and how can you keep self in check? A: The Holy Spirit in prayer. Call on the Spirit to counsel and guide you in your daily walk and to keep your focus on Christ rather than you or your circumstances.

16. Identify a few triggers that lead to taking personal control of a situation. Answers will vary.

17. How can you change your behavior or tendency to control? A: Surrender, pray God's will, not your own, especially when you're confused about something. Place your burden(s) on Him and wait for Him to guide you.

18. What are the subtle traps you frequently face? Answers may include but are not limited to: doubt, fear, temptation, confusion (no clarity), and distraction.

19. What steps do you need to take to learn surrender? A: Surrendering requires getting into the Word, prayer, and laying your life out before the Lord. Nothing is off limits to God when we truly surrender.

20. Is it possible to change what other people believe? Answers will vary.

21. Who are we responsible for? A: We are responsible for our own actions and personal decision to either accept or deny Christ as Lord and Savior.

22. What helps us stand firm? A: Christ in us.

HOW ABOUT YOU?

1. How have you tried to manage your relationship with Christ? Answers will vary.

2. Are you religious or a person of faith? Explain. Answers will vary.

3. Is your relationship with Christ more centered on His teachings or your personal experiences? Answers will vary.

4. Share a recent "Whoa, Bessie!" moment. Answers will vary.

5. Obedience comes with a price. Do you believe it leads to your demise or reward? Answers will vary.

6. Are you a *doer* or a *glorifier?* A: Doers receive reward on earth. Glorifiers receive reward in heaven following judgment day.

7. Who do you answer to in life? Answers may include myself, someone else, Christ.

8. Currently, can you say you know true joy or are you usually discontent? Answers will vary.

9. What will God reveal to you when you ask forgiveness? A: Personal sin, unresolved issues with others, the desire to serve the body.

10. Identify a holding pattern or comfort zone. Answers will vary.

11. What is the difference between Christ and Satan? A: Satan is the only one who seeks to destroy. Christ wants to restore you to Himself and guide you to the Truth in the Holy Spirit. The Holy Spirit works through our conscience and supernaturally gives us what we lack, like grace, mercy, strength, or courage.

12. What benefit could possibly come from facing personal sin? A: Forgiveness, relationships are restored, and it glorifies God.

13. Are you in conflict with someone else? Explain who. Answers will vary.

14. What comes of biblical reconciliation? A: Peace and spiritual growth/maturity.

15. What responsibility in your current conflict is your own? Answers will vary.

16. What processes do we go through by dealing with sin and who is glorified? A: Following Scripture allows the Holy Spirit to guide us to the truth of a conflict and is much more than going through the motions. Working through our sin is a cleansing process (sanctification). God is ultimately glorified.

17. How can you abide in Christ? A: Identify and use spiritual gifts to build the body.

18. What three areas of life are covered in this chapter? A: Christ or self, confessing sin, and serving God.

YOU, YOURSELF, AND HIM

1. To which laws are you bound? A: Spirit of life or sin and death.

2. What is conquered through Christ? A: Death!

3. Each day we need to do what? A: Surrender our will over to His.

4. Identify two walks of a believer. A: Blind faith versus managed, controlled, or conditional faith (which is no faith at all! It's man-made religion).

5. Can you honestly say that God has all of your heart? Answers will vary.

6. What are the two trails open to *all* creation? A: Life in Christ or death by Satan.

7. Once you've identified your walk (led by Spirit or self) and trail (un/believer), go back to paragraph two of Trail Trials and answer all of the questions, plus read 2 Peter 1:5–8 and ask yourself which of these qualities you need in order to make daily bread. Answers will vary.

8. Where does the narrow gate described by Jesus in Matthew 7:13–14 lead? A: Life.

9. Circle one: Is the Bible absolutely true, somewhat true, or not true at all? A: Absolutely true.

10. Do you have any doubt that Christ is the Son of God? Answers may vary.

11. What promise do we have in choosing salvation through Christ? A: We can stand firm in the midst of any trial and know that He is in control of all circumstances.

12. What loss has turned out to be a gain in your life? Answers will vary.

13. How do you acquire spiritual maturity? A: Lean on God for understanding. He uses tough times to grow us, to reveal, and/or to prepare us for His will.

14. How has God revealed His character in your life? Answers will vary.

15. What is off limits to God? Answers will vary.

16. Who's the drum major of your blueprints? A: Christ, self, or someone else.

17. As of today, are you able to connect the dots of your blueprints? Answers will vary.

18. Whose footprints are most visible along your blue-prints? Answers will vary.

FAITH AND THE S.T.O.P. PRINCIPLE

1. Define *faith* in Christ. A: The Bible describes faith as reliance, loyalty, or *complete trust* in God or someone else.

2. What is old and new in your testimony? Answers will vary.

3. Who has free will? A: All Creation.

4. When are believers transformed? A: Transformation happens when you choose the Spirit over your way of doing things. It's that light-bulb moment when you make the connection that living in the Spirit means you're not living for self or the world. You're bent on God, not sinfulness.

5. List three things faith requires. A: Trust, confessing sinful nature, accepting Christ as Savior.

6. What does faith in Christ proclaim? A: By our faith

in Jesus, we are acknowledging that we are sinners and that God sent the perfect sacrifice, His Son, to wipe away all our sin, to cleanse us (sanctify) in preparation to reside with God in heaven after our physical death.

7. The S.T.O.P. principle is an acronym for what? A: Surrender, trust, obedience, and patience.

SURRENDER

1. What is the opposite of surrender? A: Control.

2. To rid myself of ugly sin, I first need to: A: give complete control to God.

3. Pruning is synonymous to the trials in our lives. What does it accomplish? A: Puts our focus on Him when we surrender control.

4. What does peace accomplish? A: It is a compass believers can use to know if they are in step with God's will.

5. Circle one: Surrender is a choice or a feeling. What does it do? A: Choice. Peace increases.

6. Who does God help? A: Those who call on His name and surrender their will to His.

7. What should you do if you think you're surrendering and there's no peace? A: God is pursuing you and preparing you for a change of heart. Pray for trust in allowing Him to refine and mold you.

TRUST

1. What do surrender and trust have in common? A: Choice.

2. When/why is suffering good? Answers will vary.

3. Define hope. A: Hope is an intangible promise of God that we are His creation. He wants to rid us of our sin nature and replace it with His Spirit through faith in Christ.

4. What is the mystery of God? A: Colossians 1:27 and 2:2 reveal it is Christ living in us.

5. Why are trust and faith in Christ synonymous? A: After you personally choose to step out in faith by

believing that Christ is who He claims to be, then you begin trusting the absolute truth of the Bible.

6. Total dependence upon Christ requires _faith_ and develops _trust_ .

7. Do you fully trust God or do you need more answers? How much more understanding do you need before you do trust Him? Answers will vary.

OBEY

1. Who set the example of how to obey God? A: Christ.

2. How did this person do it? A: Jesus defines the word obedience with His life, death, resurrection, and promise to return to claim all believers as His own.

3. What are the ingredients of an OMS? A: Obedience is the meat between two pieces of trust bread.

4. Does God ask us to do the impossible? A: God does not ask us to say or do anything (1) we can't handle

(1 Corinthians 10:13) and that (2) Jesus didn't already accomplish ahead of us (John 17:4; 19:28).

5. Who will resurrect all sinners who claim Christ as Savior? A: The Holy Spirit is in all believers and has the power to raise us from the dead at Christ's return.

6. List a few of the fruits of obedience. A: Love, joy, peace, patience, kindness, goodness, faithfulness, gentleness, and self-control (Galatians 5:22–23).

PATIENCE

1. What does patience follow? A: An act of obedience.

2. If obedience and trust make the sandwich, then what adds flavor? A: A generous amount of patience.

3. How did Esther handle conflict? A: Esther fasted and prayed for deliverance while asking Mordecai and their people to join her petition.

4. How did God respond? A: He answered Esther's prayers by granting a meeting with the king and

Haman. The story ends with Haman being publicly hung at the same gallows he built to use on Mordecai and others who would not submissively bow to him. The Jews were delivered from going to slaughter.

5. Discuss a couple of ways you can wisely use your spare time. Answers may include getting into the Word and prayer.

6. In between answered prayer, what are some things God is doing for patient believers? A: His Word says he is either busy working behind the scenes or working *in* us to make the necessary heart changes so He can work *through* us to accomplish His will!

7. What can you do if you feel God has *not* heard your prayers? A: Surrender your circumstances again, be still, and stand firm.

8. Is there a step we must take in order for our faith to increase? A: Yes! Step out in faith!

CONCLUSION: WALKING SHOES FIT FOR A NARROW PATH!

1. Who leads the narrow path? A: Jesus

2. What did He leave in His wake? A: Living bread and water.

3. You forfeit _peace_ when you try to control your circumstances.

4. What exercises will help you learn patience? A: Prayer and quiet time with the Lord. Also, read the Bible.

5. Who has paid the price for your shoes? A: Answers may vary.

6. Share with your group the path you have chosen and how you plan to stay on course. Answers will vary.

BIBLIOGRAPHY

Comfort, Ray. *What Hollywood Believes: An Intimate Look at the Faith of the Famous.* Towson: Genesis Publishing, 2004.

Gilbert, Dr. Larry. *Team Ministry Spiritual Gifts Based Ministry.* 2009. http://www.TeamMinistry.com (accessed February 2009).

Goodrick, Edward W., and John R. Kohlenberger III. *New International Bible Concordance.* Zondervan.

Graham, Franklin. "Building on the Foundations of Faith." *Samaritan's Purse Operation Christmas Child Special Report,* January 2009: 15.

Life Application Study Bible, NIV. Wheaton: Tyndale House Publishers, Inc., 1998, 1989, 1990, 1991, 1993, 1996, 2004, 2005.

Samra, Senior Pastor Jim. "Keep the Sabbath #22." *For audio go to www.calvary-church.net.* Grand Rapids: Calvary Church, March 1, 2009.

The American Heritage Dictionary of the English Language, third edition. Houghton Mifflin Company.

Towner, Daniel B., and John H. Sammis. *Trust and Obey.* 1887.

Walter C. Kaiser, Jr., and Duane Garrett. *Archaeological Study Bible, NIV.* Grand Rapids: Zondervan, 2006.

Woodward, Jeanne, and Bonnie Damon. "Housing Characteristics: 2000, Census 2000 Brief." *2000 Census Bureau.* October 2001 (accessed March 2009).

|LIVE

listen|imagine|view|experience

ALSO AVAILABLE IN AUDIO BOOK FORMAT!

In addition to the paper version, this title is also available in an abridged audio book format. Enjoy listening to this title through either a complete CD package, with cover and disc artwork, or download to your computer as a digital file and within minutes you can listen to the book through your computer's speakers, burn it to an audio CD, or save the file to your portable music device (such as Apple's popular iPod) and listen on the go!

To order please visit www.tatepublishing.com/bookstore or www.thestopprinciple.com.